ENCHANTED BY
VIETNAM

COOKING AND TRAVELLING WITH QUYÊN

CONTENTS

FOREWORD **5**

ENCHANTED BY VIETNAM **7**

A PORTRAIT OF TRUONG THI QUYÊN **10**

VIETNAMESE CUISINE
IN A NUTSHELL **24**

DIFFERENCES BETWEEN NORTH, SOUTH AND
CENTRAL VIETNAM **26**

A JOURNEY OF FLAVOURS THROUGH VIETNAM **27**

SAPA **28**

HANOI **38**

HA LONG BAY **58**

NINH BINH **68**

HUE **80**

HOI AN **100**

QUY NHON **114**

HO CHI MINH CITY **136**

CAN THO **152**

PHU QUOC **164**

BASIC RECIPES **178**

THE FLAVOURS OF VIETNAM **180**

INDEX **188**

ACKNOWLEDGEMENTS **190**

COLOPHON **191**

ONG BA NOI, MY GRANDPARENTS ON MY FATHER'S SIDE, WERE FISHERMEN.
ONG BA NGOAI, MY GRANDPARENTS ON MY MOTHER'S SIDE, WERE FARMERS.

THEY WORKED HARD, EVERY DAY, FROM EARLY MORNING TILL LATE AT NIGHT.
EVERY DAY THEY MADE SURE THERE WAS FRESH FISH, RICE AND VEGETABLES.
THEY SAY THAT I GREW UP IN A CULINARY WORLD.

As a child I always looked forward to the Remembrance of the Dead. This remains a very special tradition. On that day all the uncles and aunts get up very early to slaughter chickens, ducks and pigs. The aunts cook the tastiest dishes and desserts, often the favourite food of the dead. When they are finished cooking they place all the food on an altar. The eldest, grandpa, prays first, followed by the others. After an hour, once the incense has gone out, we eat the food together. Even in Belgium it is a tradition we continue to uphold. Praying for the dead means that we never forget our roots. It is also the moment when we all get together - family, friends, neighbours - to catch up. Food is very important to the Vietnamese. It brings people together to eat and discuss the events of the day. To exchange news and swap stories.

Food has been the common thread throughout my life. It has always been important. In the past, when I had to take care of my siblings, and now because I like to pamper the guests in my restaurant.

I believe in the words of the Vietnamese Buddhist Zen master Thich Nhat Hanh: nothing survives without proper nutrition. I am constantly looking for pure and healthy ingredients.

When my family and guests of Little Asia have had a good meal and are happy, then I also feel truly happy. It gives me satisfaction and positive energy.
It motivates me to carry on.

Enjoy my book.
Enjoy the delicious and healthy food.
Enjoy our story as boat refugees living in Belgium.

Thank you.

Quyên

ENCHANTED BY VIETNAM

A coup de foudre is probably the best way to describe my introduction to Vietnam. It happened somewhere in Hanoi, in one of the small streets of the old town. It was just gone six o'clock in the morning. Men and women were eating Pho seated on small plastic chairs. They slurped and clicked with their chopsticks and, above all, they chattered non-stop.

The humidity was overwhelming. And we were fatigued from our flight the night before. But we were hungry. And although soup is not generally the first thing we would want in the morning, we were seduced by the friendly lady beckoning us. Ten minutes later we were slurping along with the Vietnamese. Was it because of the heavenly Pho? Or the hospitality and laughter of our neighbours? Or was it the simple setting and the purity of the ingredients? I cannot really put my finger on it, but somehow, at that very moment, Vietnam changed my life.

On previous trips to Asia we had acquainted ourselves extensively with Thai, Cambodian and Laotian cuisine. We believed we had discovered the apex of Asian cuisine years ago in Thailand. Nothing could have been further from the truth. Vietnam is the absolute Mecca for lovers of healthy and tasty food. Vietnamese cuisine is honest, pure and always fresh. No complicated techniques, no difficult ingredients. And above all, perfectly balanced. Always complete with sufficient vitamins, minerals, proteins and carbohydrates. Always a harmony of sweet and sour, crunchy and soft, hot and cold. Lots of herbs and spices. No additives or chemicals.

The Vietnamese are meticulous about their food. And about their health. A study by the World Health Organization in the 70s showed that the Vietnamese - even after the Vietnam War and the horrors they had endured - were the healthiest people in the world. That was no accident. So these days, with so many of us obsessed with healthy diets and a healthy lifestyle, Vietnamese cuisine can be a great source of inspiration. And if you are lucky enough to have Truong Thi Quyên as your hostess, then you are particularly privileged.

Quyên, Gwen for non-Vietnamese, is the owner of and driving force behind the renowned restaurant Little Asia in Brussels. Born and raised in Vietnam, she came to Belgium at the age of fourteen and one cannot imagine a more enthusiastic and passionate ambassador for her homeland and its food. You can read the story of this inspiring woman's life further on. Our collaboration in writing this book was as enjoyable as it was productive. Simply because she speaks with so much love about everything. And I hope that this comes across in the stories and the recipes.

Vietnam and Quyên have changed my life. The nostalgia, the urge to go back again and again - to Vietnam or to Little Asia - has only grown since writing this book. Hopefully it will inspire you, too.

I wish you a pleasant and tasty journey!

Sylvie

Sylvie D'Hoore (42) is a freelance journalist. She shares a passion for Vietnam with Quyên and enjoyed immensely the job of moulding the numerous stories and anecdotes Quyên told about her country into this book.

I'VE BEEN VERY LUCKY IN MY LIFE

TRUONG THI QUYÊN

She beams when she speaks. She laughs a lot and giggles occasionally. She has endless stories to tell. Stories full of wisdom. Anecdotes that show how and why she became who she is today. It is no coincidence that it was Quyên who succeeded in setting up the successful Vietnamese restaurant Little Asia in Brussels. The job required great perseverance, humility and grace. Trial and error, time and time again. But always with a tremendous drive and passion. If you ever end up eating there, or when you are preparing one of the recipes in this book, take some time to reflect upon this incredible woman's extraordinary story.

Quyên: "One day I was cycling with my youngest brother Hai to the market. Along the way there was someone selling snails, a delicacy in Vietnam. My brother begged me to buy some snails for him. But I had to be tough. If I had done that, the rest of the family would have had nothing to eat that night. He cried rivers of tears. I was twelve years old and it broke my heart."

ABANDONED ON THE BEACH "I was nine years old when my father left us behind in Vietnam. I was waiting as usual on the beach for the fish he had caught that night. But he did not return that evening. Nor the following day. Every day I went back to look for him, but to no avail. It was said that he - like many Vietnamese after the Vietnam War - had fled by boat. But I did not understand that. Why? Moreover, we were not allowed to talk about it because the police were very hard on boat people. And their families. My mom was angry and sad. She was left behind with six children.

RESPONSIBILITY "As far back as I can remember, I was never able to play as a child. I always had to take care of my siblings. I had to wash them, do the housework, fetch water from the well... We all had two garments each, which had to be washed every night so we could wear them again the next day. At nine years old I was a housewife and I cooked for the whole family. My oldest brother Nghia caught fish, while my sister minded the children. But as the eldest girl I carried the greatest responsibility. Sometimes I still dream of that time and I see our home and our lives. In the house there was a chest where mom kept our money. Sometimes

We were also worried sick. Was he still alive? Was he dead? Had he drowned? Or died of hunger? After twelve days we received a letter from Singapore in which he wrote that he had fled and had been rescued by a Belgian boat. Vietnam offered him no future. He would find a safe haven for us in Belgium. His message was a huge relief. But also a disappointment. Because now we had to manage on our own. When would we see him again? Would we ever see him again? That experience changed me forever."

I had to take a little out to buy food. I was always extremely careful. I was afraid that burglars would come and steal the money, because it was all we had. In Vietnam, it is not customary to lock your door. But I barricaded our door with a chair so that I would wake up if anyone ever attempted to get in."

"One day the box was empty, the money had run out. I cycled to my grandfather's house, seven kilometres into the countryside. I was given a bowl of rice and was allowed to take some vegetables from the garden so that I would be able to feed the family. When his rice also ran out I picked chilli peppers and sold them at the market. With that

// Together with my parents and daughter Claudia

money I could then buy other food. I've always been resourceful."

"When my grandfather and my uncles returned from the sea they had back pain from the hard work on the boat. I often gave them back and neck massages, for which I was sometimes given a little money. Other children sometimes bought sweets with their pocket money but I never did. I saved everything. Or I bought a kilo of sweets and a kilo of fruit, set up a stall outside our house and sold the sweets and the fruit again, thereby creating my own little shop. I gave the proceeds to my mother to buy food. I was always terrified that we would not have enough, that we would starve. I was driven by a survival instinct. I wanted to help my mother. I saw her suffering. I often wondered when my mother actually slept. Whenever it was too hot she would wave a fan above us so that her six children could sleep. I pretended I was asleep but I watched her constantly."

"The sadness, the anger, the powerlessness of those two people, my father and my mother. How could I, as a child, ever understand that?"

UTTER GRIEF "I've cried a lot in my life. My mom was angry with my dad for a long time after he left us. Then they started writing to each other. But my mom could not read or write that well, so I had to help her. Sometimes she would wake me in the middle of the night to read a letter to her. Or sometimes she dictated what to write. Often words of regret and sadness. Tears rolled down my cheeks. The sadness, the anger, the powerlessness of those two people, my father and my mother. How could I, as a child, ever understand that?"

"One day I cycled with my youngest brother to the market. Along the way there was someone selling snails, a delicacy in Vietnam. My brother begged me to buy snails for him. But I had to be tough. If I had done that, the rest of the family would have had nothing to eat that night. He cried rivers of tears. I was twelve years old and it broke my heart."

THE GREAT DREAM "I arrived in Belgium on June 18 1986. I was fourteen. The dream of every Vietnamese had come true for us. We had made it! But everything was strange to us. The people, the houses, the language... We thought our dad had everything here, but he had nothing. Up until our arrival he had lived with the pastor of the East Flemish town of Wichelen, but with six kids and a wife this was no longer possible. So he had to rent a house. For 7000 francs a month. Everything was broken in the house but the people of Wichelen came to help fix the place up. For the first week we went to eat at neighbours and friends. Everyone welcomed us with open arms. Dad had to take a week off work to be with us. But then normal life resumed and he went back to work. We sat at home. It was almost holiday time and so we couldn't go to school. We did not understand the language. Every time the bell rang we were terrified. We wept for a whole month. Out of homesickness. Was this the land of our dreams?"

"Our dad was angry. One evening he called us together: 'I risked my life for you. I managed to buy seven plane tickets to get you here. There was no future in Vietnam. All you do now is complain. I'm not rich but I brought you to a free country. I have no house, no car, I have nothing. But you are young. You can study, you can make your own future. It is your choice.' This truly was a wake-up call. Six months later I was speaking Dutch."

PERFECTIONISM "To earn some money, I started cleaning. I had always done this in Vietnam, but our house there was much smaller and it was not terribly clean. I was soon told that I was not doing it right. I panicked. I was afraid that I would never be good enough. From that moment on I decided to always do my very best at everything, everywhere. And to do everything as perfectly as possible. That is not always easy.

Perfection does not exist, but I have tried hard to get close to it. To follow my dream. And to do whatever it took to achieve it. I was given a wonderful opportunity by my father. I wanted to take advantage of that opportunity."

SCHOOL AND STUDIES "The religion teacher who had helped my father, helped me too. He taught me how to conduct myself. And that I should keep my mouth shut when eating. It might seem trivial, but to me it was all new. When school started again in September I had to start sixth grade of primary school as a fourteen-year-old in order to master the language. I only had a Vietnamese-Dutch dictionary to help me. But it worked. I was good at maths, physics and chemistry. I then went on to study industrial science in Wetteren. To earn money, I worked as a dishwasher at a nearby restaurant on weekends and had to cycle back to Wichelen at three in the morning. Sometimes when it was snowing. Sometimes I had groceries with me and I fell off the bike. But I never complained. I had to go on. I would never have gotten to where I am today without experiencing a few difficult moments.

That's how I was raised. Humble, tolerant, accepting. If you are a guest of Vietnamese people, the first thing they ask is: "Have you eaten? Please, take a seat." Even though they may not have enough for everyone. Even when they will have to do without themselves. Caring for others comes naturally. Sometimes I think I should enjoy myself more. I do not want to be like my mother. But subconsciously I seem to be becoming more and more like her. My mother took care of her brothers, sisters, children and grandchildren her entire life. Sometimes she was so exhausted she couldn't even eat. But when she saw that others were enjoying themselves she was happy. And she still is.

I have become like her. I take care of my children, my husband, my clients. Sometimes I am exhausted. But when I see that I can make other people happy I regain my energy."

FROM MANGA TO VIETNAMESE SPRING ROLLS "I had sworn that I would never get into the catering business. For years I had worked in a restaurant and heard my boss complaining about profits, overheads and his hard life. There was always something wrong. I did not want that. I wanted a carefree life. But blood is thicker than water, right? It wasn't easy, however. People are happy to hire Asians because they are hard workers. Because they are accommodating and do not complain. But there wasn't much work for us. I would have done anything. Stock supermarket shelves, work in a clothing store... But I was never hired. When I got married I did not want to be dependent on my husband. I wanted to work as well. When we were on honeymoon in Hong Kong I saw how successful manga (Japanese comics, ed.) were. That gave me an idea. I filled a whole suitcase and sold them when I got back to Brussels. When the manga turned out to be a great success I opened a shop next to the restaurant. After 5 years the manga hype had fizzled out and my sister Hanh continued the business alone. I opened a new business. An Asian snack bar with quick bites and a range of Asian food. The place was full in no time. Everyone wanted to be there. The food was tasty, the girls were friendly and the atmosphere was good. I was happy."

"Our snack bar gradually turned into a restaurant. It was only open until six o'clock, but customers began asking whether I could stay open a little longer. Some said: why not start a real restaurant? A real Vietnamese restaurant that is accessible to everyone.

But I had never been to an upscale Vietnamese restaurant myself. Little by little I began to believe in the project. I wanted a new concept, something that did not exist anywhere else. I went to London, Frankfurt and Paris and visited all kinds of Vietnamese restaurants. But I did not find any inspiration. I was looking for the authenticity of Vietnam but then in a modern setting. I eventually hired an architect and we worked the whole concept out in shades of purple and pink. The first customers and the press were very enthusiastic. In reviews, journalists wondered whether they were in Hong Kong or Paris. I've been very lucky in my life. God must like me. I believe in fate. There are no coincidences. Things happen because they are meant to happen."

STEWS AND HORSE STEAK "I get up early so that I can chat with my daughter or son for a while. Then I do some paperwork at home before driving to Little Asia. After the afternoon shift I drive home to cook the evening meal. Some people think I'm crazy. Why do you go home to cook? Don't you have a restaurant? But if I bring home food that was cooked in the afternoon, by six o'clock it's no longer very tasty. I sometimes bring home a piece of meat, but I always cook fresh. I do not cook Vietnamese food every day. My children were born here. They enjoy Belgian food. We eat Vietnamese food two or three times a week and Belgian food the rest of the time. Half and half, so to speak. I love Belgian cuisine. I love fried fish, steamed fish, fish in the oven, chicken in the oven, beef stew... and even horse meat!

Some people say that Belgian cuisine is too heavy. But you can always decide for yourself how much cream or butter you use."

GOALS AND DREAMS "I have no major goal in my life. I have no big dreams. I want a job and a house. And I want my family to be happy. That is the most important thing to me. I might have achieved a lot - essentially I have it all: a beautiful house, a car, nice clothes - but I want the people around me to do well, too. I continue to feel responsible. I work hard, 16 to 18 hours a day. Sometimes I think that I should slow down a bit. But I can't, as my staff also need to earn enough to allow their children to study. I can't deny them that. I am nothing without my team. They have been loyal to me for sixteen years. If I stop, they'll be out on the street and will have to start from scratch again. I don't want that. Recently someone said to me: in Vietnam you definitely would have made it as well. But I'm not so sure. I see people who work just as hard as me but have nothing. That bothers me. We return to Vietnam every year. Which is great. But it's also difficult sometimes. People there think that we live in paradise. They all expect something from me. And I'm not tough enough to say no. I am fond of these people. They helped me when we were struggling. They gave me food and shelter in Saigon. So I hand out twenty or fifty euros every now and then. The last time I was there I gave away a few thousand euros. Some people tell me I shouldn't do that. You have to teach people how to make it on their own. I've tried that. I bought the uncle who did so much for me a fishing boat. But he can't use that boat to fish in the area any more because all the fish have been caught already. And he can't go further out to sea. The boat is now just sitting there. I can't give everyone a shop or set them up for the rest of their lives. I can only make them happy for a brief moment or two."

"I'm at my happiest when I'm sitting at the table with my husband and children, when I can hug my children and when my restaurant is full. Then I just light up."

"When I enter the restaurant everyone looks at me. Or they wait to greet me. That's a great feeling and one that I almost can't fathom. It gives me the energy and strength to go on. I love to spoil my guests, to introduce them to the flavours of my wonderful country. Vietnamese cuisine is often underestimated. Everyone talks a lot about other Asian cuisines but in Vietnam everything is so fresh, so pure and so delicious. These days people try to maintain a healthy, balanced diet. And I can tell you: Vietnamese cuisine has it all. It makes me very proud of my country."

VIETNAMESE CUISINE IN A NUTSHELL

RICE

Rice is the national treasure of the Vietnamese. A meal without rice is unthinkable and there are many different types of grains. Not to mention rice noodles, rice flakes, rice paper, rice vermicelli, rice flour, rice liqueur...

VEGETABLES

Vietnamese people eat lots of vegetables. Not like we do - served separately - but incorporated in the dishes and so with a greater variety. The freshness of the vegetables is also very important.

MEAT, FISH AND SHELLFISH

Vietnamese people love meat and fish, although one should try not to overdo it. Meat should preferably be cut into very thin slices or be as pure as possible. With bones to chew on and a little fat for that extra juicy flavour.
Depending on the region, there is usually no shortage of fish and shellfish.

FRESH HERBS AND SPICES

Almost every Vietnamese dish is accompanied by a bowl of fresh herbs: coriander, mint, Asian basil, shiso, spring onion... The choice varies from region to region and from dish to dish. The herbs, which are often rolled into a bundle before each bite, provide extra flavour and extra vitamins and minerals. Spices like cinnamon, ginger, lemongrass, cardamom and cloves also give extra colour to the dishes.

FISH SAUCE

Fish sauce (nuoc mam) is indispensable to Vietnamese cuisine. Some find the smell initially very penetrating, but it can add a lot of flavour to a dish. Vietnamese fish sauce is also very pure and healthy because it consists of seventy-five per cent freshly caught anchovies.

BALANCE

Vietnamese cuisine is very balanced. Each dish has its own yin and yang. Each texture, flavour and method has a counterpart: crispy and soft, hot and cold, sweet and savoury, raw and cooked...

DIFFERENCES
BETWEEN NORTH,
SOUTH AND CENTRAL
VIETNAM

The term Vietnamese cuisine is something of a misnomer, actually. The country is far too vast and the culinary differences between north, south and central Vietnam too large to put them all under one umbrella.

Many of the most famous Vietnamese dishes (like Pho) have their origins in the north, including a lot of the stews and soups because it's colder there. In the north, the cooking is also more traditional and more rigid in its use of herbs and ingredients.

In central Vietnam they prefer small side dishes and the flavours are also hotter and spicier. The region also has the widest selection of dishes and the best ingredients, thanks in part to the emperor who lived for years in Hue and was responsible for cultivating a very sophisticated and delicious cuisine. The region also boasts the largest selection of vegetarian dishes, which were first introduced by the Buddhists.

The cuisine in the south of Vietnam was influenced by Southern-Chinese immigrants and French settlers. Southerners tend to prefer a sweeter flavour and use a wider range of herbs.

A JOURNEY OF FLAVOURS THROUGH
VIETNAM

Ten cities, countless flavours. Explore Vietnam from north to south and let yourself be
inspired both culinarily and culturally by this wonderful country.

Sapa

SAPA

Paddy fields in all shapes and sizes, terraces as far as the eye can see and a beautiful, multi-layered palette of green. Unmistakably Sapa.

Sapa is the name of the province and also of the most famous mountain town in the north of Vietnam. If you love nature, pristineness and purity you will feel right at home here. The region is no longer a hidden gem, the area attracts hundreds of thousands of tourists annually. But as soon as you step off the beaten path you're all alone in a breathtaking setting where traditional mountain people provide a colourful spectacle with their authentic costumes. You can walk for hours and enjoy the peace, tranquillity and simplicity. Sapa is undoubtedly one of the most beautiful regions of Vietnam.

Quyên: "Fifteen years ago, when my restaurant had just opened and we had many guests for dinner, everyone talked about Sapa. But I had never even heard of Sapa! I was quite embarrassed. As a Vietnamese I did not even know my own country. I was even afraid to ask where it was! I lived in Vietnam until I was fourteen but I had never strayed beyond my hometown Quy Nhon and hadn't even been to Saigon."

"IN SAPA THE FLAVOURS OF THE DISHES ARE AS INTENSE AS THE BEAUTIFUL SURROUNDINGS."

"When I visited Sapa for the first time in 2002 we ate on the side of the road from a woman cooking on a charcoal fire. She prepared a grilled bird for us, with sweet potato and sticky rice on a bamboo stick. At first it sounded a bit strange, but it was a good choice because the grilled bird tasted superb.
The cuisine of Sapa is very simple. Everything is cooked on charcoal fires, but the flavours are as intense as the beautiful surroundings."

CHIM CUT NUONG
GRILLED QUAIL

2 quails, boned
1 stalk of lemongrass, finely chopped
1 shallot, finely chopped
2 garlic cloves, crushed
3 lime leaves, finely chopped
1 tbsp honey
2 tbsp fish sauce
1 tsp light soy sauce
1 tbsp vegetable oil
½ tsp five-spice powder
½ tsp turmeric powder
Sea salt

SERVES 2
25 MINUTES + MARINATING TIME

Preheat the oven to 180° C.

Make a marinade of lemongrass, turmeric powder, five-spice powder, soy sauce, fish sauce, oil, honey, garlic, lime leaves and shallots. Season with a pinch of sea salt. Brush the quail with this mixture. Allow to marinate for at least 2 hours (or overnight) covered in the refrigerator for more flavour.

Transfer the quail and spices to a baking dish. Place in the oven for 10 to 12 minutes until fully cooked. Turn them after 5 to 6 minutes so that both sides become brown.

You can also fry the quail in a pan with oil or on the barbecue.

You can replace the quail with chicken.

THIT NUONG THAN HOA
BARBECUE MEAT

1 kg spare ribs
1 kg chicken wings
6 chicken thighs
10 lime leaves, finely chopped

FOR THE MARINADE

6 stalks of lemongrass,
finely chopped
6 stalks of spring onion,
finely chopped
2 shallots, finely chopped
1 bulb of garlic, crushed
6 tbsp fish sauce
2 tbsp honey
1 tbsp vegetable oil
1 tsp brown sugar
2 tsp sea salt

SERVE WITH

Fish sauce vinaigrette
Herb salad
(see basic recipe pages 178-179)

SERVES 4-6
20 MINUTES + MARINATING TIME

Cut the ribs into pieces, rinse and pat dry with kitchen paper.

Mix all the ingredients for the marinade in a large bowl. Leave the meat to marinate in this mixture for 1 to 2 hours (or overnight) covered in the fridge.

After marinating the meat, sprinkle it with the lime leaves and fry on the barbecue.

CA TIM XAO HANH

STEWED AUBERGINES

1 aubergine, sliced
1 shallot, finely chopped
3 stalks of spring onion,
finely chopped
(white and green separated)
2 garlic cloves, crushed
1 tbsp light soy sauce
1 tsp sesame oil
2 tbsp vegetable oil
Sea salt

SERVES 2
10 MINUTES

Fry the garlic, shallot and white part of the spring onion in oil. Add the slices of aubergine.

Pour in 100 ml of water and cover. Leave to simmer, stirring frequently. If necessary, add extra water.

Once the aubergines are soft and cooked, season them with soy sauce, sea salt, the green part of the spring onion and sesame oil. Then remove immediately from the heat.

You can finish off this dish with toasted sesame seeds or toasted pumpkin seeds.

Hanoi

HANOI

You either love it or you hate it. This is a statement that certainly applies to Hanoi. The hustle and bustle of the Vietnamese capital may put some people off, but if you look further you'll find a city to fall in love with.

Hanoi is quite unlike other major cities. No matter how busy, the atmosphere is always relaxed and charming. Daily life revolves around Hoan Kiem lake, which acts as the heart connecting the various neighbourhoods together. In the mornings and evenings the inhabitants of the Vietnamese capital gather here for their daily Tai Chi sessions. The honking of thousands of scooters disappears naturally into the background.

The Old Quarter, Hanoi's old neighbourhood, in particular is home to a fascinating maze of streets lined with food stalls in all shapes and sizes. Each neighbourhood has its own specialty: from noodle soup with beef (Pho Bo) to steamed rice with mushrooms (Banh cuon) or grilled bacon with rice vermicelli and green herbs (bun cha). You shouldn't expect too much from the facilities. Tiny plastic stools serve as both table and chair, packed close together under a tarp in case a rainstorm breaks; chopsticks bundled in large glasses and little napkins for messy eaters. But in return for this simple setting you will be served a heavenly meal.

Quyên: "Hanoi is the walhalla of street food. And there is no better food to be had than that which is served on the street at the many stalls. It all starts very early in the morning. The Vietnamese do not eat breakfast at home in Hanoi but immediately take to the streets. Eating is a social event. Even at six o'clock in the morning. A bowl of Pho Bo will easily get you through the day. The hot broth with beef and herbs provides plenty of energy. The fresh herbs mixed through it provide extra flavour and vitamins. Every Vietnamese meal is perfectly balanced."

"HANOI IS THE WALHALLA OF STREET FOOD. THERE IS NO BETTER FOOD TO BE HAD THAN THAT WHICH IS SERVED ON THE STREET."

TEA:

A MOMENT OF RELAXATION

"Vietnamese people drink tea every day. It is an ancient tradition that is seen primarily as a way to relax and have a little chat or enjoy the shade of a tree or sit on the street with friends. Drinking tea together is a bonding experience. Pouring tea is a sign of hospitality."

PHO:
WHAT'S IN
A NAME

Quyên: "The north of Vietnam is colder than the south. That's why more stews, pot-au-feu, are made there. Vietnamese women carry bamboo poles on their shoulders with baskets at both ends. On one side are fresh herbs, bowls and spoons. On the other side a fire for cooking the broth. During the colonial period the French would point to the women and shout "Feu, feu..., fire, fire." The Vietnamese adopted the word and named their broth Pho (Feu)."

PHO BO

NOODLE SOUP WITH BEEF

FOR THE BROTH

800 g beef shank
1 onion, peeled
1 shallot
3 tbsp fish sauce
50 g fresh ginger
3 black cardamom pods or cloves
6 star anise
2 cinnamon sticks
1 tsp brown sugar
3 tsp sea salt

FOR THE SOUP

100 g beef, in thin slices
300 g rice noodles
(fresh or dried)
1 onion, in rings
4 stalks of spring onion, julienned
6 sprigs of coriander
(stems and leaves separated)
1 handful of Asian basil leaves*

* optional

SERVES 4
120 MINUTES

FOR THE BROTH

Bring 3 litres of water to the boil. Add the beef shank and season with 1 teaspoon of sea salt. Add the onion (whole).

Cut the shallots and ginger in half and crush with the flat side of a cleaver. Add to the broth and season with the rest of the salt, cinnamon sticks, cardamom and star anise. Leave to simmer partially covered for 2 hours on a low heat.

Remove the foam from the broth at regular intervals. After 2 hours, add the coriander stalks, fish sauce and sugar.

THE SOUP

Soak the dried rice noodles for 15 minutes in lukewarm water (not necessary with fresh rice noodles). Remove the noodles from the water and cook until tender. Drain and divide among four bowls.

In the meantime, remove the beef shank from the soup and cut into thin slices. Add to the noodles, together with the slices of raw beef.

Mix the onion rings with the coriander leaves, Asian basil and spring onion. Add this herb mixture to the bowls.

Bring the broth back to the boil and spoon enough of it into the bowls so that the raw beef can continue cooking.

You can grill the shallots and ginger in advance for extra flavour.

Lovers of spicy food can add chopped chilli peppers.

BANH CUON

RICE PANCAKE FILLED WITH MEAT AND MUSHROOMS

FOR THE DOUGH

200 g rice flour
or banh cuon flour
½ tsp sea salt

FOR THE STUFFING

150 g lean bacon, chopped
4 dried black mushrooms
or shiitake
3 shallots in half rings
4 stalks of spring onion,
finely chopped
1 tbsp fish sauce
3 tbsp vegetable oil
Ground black pepper and sea salt

SERVE WITH

Fish sauce vinaigrette
Herb salad
(see basic recipe pages 178-179)

SERVES 4 (SNACK)
SERVES 2 (MAIN)
60 MINUTES + 30 MINUTES SOAKING

Let the dried mushrooms soak in hot water for 30 minutes and drain (shiitake mushrooms do not need soaking). Finely chop the mushrooms.

Make the pancake batter using 400 ml of water, the flour and half a teaspoon of sea salt. Stir well in a large mixing bowl.

Sauté 1 shallot in 1 tablespoon of oil on a high heat. After about 1 minute add the bacon and stir-fry.

Stir in the chopped mushrooms and pour in the fish sauce. Season to taste with salt and pepper. Garnish with spring onion and remove immediately from the heat so that it stays nicely green.

Fry the remaining shallots in the rest of the oil until golden brown and crispy. Drain on kitchen paper and retain the oil from the pan.

Heat a little oil from the shallots in a pancake pan. Spoon in some dough and fry the wafer-thin pancakes, one by one. Cover while cooking (you do not have to turn the pancakes). Place the pancakes on a plate as soon as they are ready.

Spread the filling over the pancakes and roll them up.

Serve with herb salad, fish sauce vinaigrette and the fried shallots.

For the filling you can replace the bacon with chicken. Or leave out the meat to make vegetarian pancakes.

NEM

QUYÊN: "NEMS ARE VIETNAMESE SPRING ROLLS, BUT THEY ARE ALSO MUCH MORE THAN THAT. EVERY BITE YOU TAKE OF A NEM IS A MEAL IN ITSELF BECAUSE NEMS ARE MADE OF RICE PAPER, VERMICELLI, VEGETABLES AND MEAT AND SERVED WITH FRESH HERBS AND A DIPPING SAUCE.

For a healthy, balanced meal each ingredient is essential. This is definitely one of my favourite dishes. Without the herbs I can eat a maximum of three or four. With the herbs I can eat ten or more. I like to roll up the herbs - lettuce, mint, coriander, shiso, cucumber... all those fresh flavours! And then there's the crispiness of the fried rice paper. Yummy! Be sure not to forget the fish sauce vinaigrette (recipe on page 178), which is indispensable in Vietnamese cuisine. The taste is both sweet and sour thanks to the lime juice and sugar. But without it the nems are incomplete. Vietnamese dishes are very subtle. The addition of the dip sauce gives you more flavour. In Europe, we often use unhealthy mayonnaise, tartar or pickles as our dip. Vietnamese dipping sauce is pure and natural, and very healthy given that it's packed with proteins. Nems combine a variety of tastes and nuances: sweet, sour, cold, hot, crispy, soft... "

If you ever go looking for nems in Vietnam, you should remember the following: in the north they are called Nem ran, in the south they are called Cha gio.

NEM / CHA GIO

VIETNAMESE SPRING ROLLS WITH MEAT AND VEGETABLES

200 g lean pork, boned and ground with the machine

1 handful of soybean vermicelli

20 rice sheets (squares of 17 cm)

8 shiitake mushrooms or button mushrooms, finely chopped

100 g bean sprouts

50 g carrots, grated

1 onion, finely chopped

1 stalk of spring onion, finely chopped

2 tbsp fish sauce

Ground black pepper and sea salt

SERVE WITH

Fish sauce vinaigrette

Herb salad

(see basic recipe pages 178-179)

20 ROLLS

30 MINUTES

Soak the soybean vermicelli in hot water for 5 minutes, drain and cut into short pieces.

Preheat the deep fryer to 180° C.

Put the meat in a large bowl along with the soaked soybean vermicelli, bean sprouts, carrots, shiitake mushrooms, onion and spring onion. Season with fish sauce, pepper and sea salt. Mix and knead everything together so that the ingredients become one whole.

Soak the rice sheets very briefly in hot water until soft. Put them on a damp towel or plate with a point facing down. Add a tablespoon of filling and roll up to the middle. Fold in the sides and roll up.

First fry the nems for 2 to 3 minutes in the deep fryer. Allow to drain on kitchen paper before frying for a second time for an extra crispy crust.

Roll the nems in a lettuce leaf with coriander and mint and dip them in the fish sauce vinaigrette.

Make as many nems as you like, fry them once and keep the ones you don't eat in the freezer for later.

You can replace the pork with chicken, crab, scampi...

CHA CA

FRIED SEA BREAM FILLET AND DILL

4 sea bream fillets with skin
(120 g/fillet), diced

200 g rice vermicelli

4 stalks of spring onion,
finely chopped
(white and green separated)

2 shallots, finely chopped

4 tbsp dill, chopped

4 tbsp unsalted, roasted peanuts,
chopped

2 tbsp fish sauce

2 tbsp vegetable oil

1 tsp turmeric powder

1 tsp brown sugar

Ground black pepper and sea salt

SERVE WITH

Fish sauce vinaigrette
Herb salad
(see basic recipe pages 178-179)

SERVES 4
20 MINUTES

Soak the rice vermicelli in warm water for 15 minutes. Remove from the water and boil for 1 minute. Drain.

Season the fish cubes in a bowl with turmeric, fish sauce, sugar, black pepper and a pinch of sea salt. Add the shallot, the white part of the spring onions and 1 tablespoon of oil.

Fry this fish mixture in the remaining oil with the skin side up. Turn the fish cubes when the underside has turned golden brown. When the fish is cooked, add the dill and the green part of the spring onions. Remove immediately from the heat.

Sprinkle over the peanuts and serve with rice vermicelli, herb salad and fish sauce vinaigrette.

You can replace the sea bream fillet with salmon, mackerel, sole...

BUN CHA

GRILLED PORK BELLY WITH RICE VERMICELLI

150 g pork belly, sliced

100 g pork belly,
diced as tartar

100 g rice vermicelli

1 shallot, finely chopped

4 stalks of spring onion,
finely chopped

2 garlic cloves, crushed

2 tsp fish sauce

2 tbsp vegetable oil

1 tsp brown sugar

Ground black pepper and sea salt

SERVE WITH

Fish sauce vinaigrette
Herb salad
(see basic recipe pages 178-179)

SERVES 2
45 MINUTES

Put the two types of meat into two separate bowls.

Divide the shallots, fish sauce, sugar, spring onion, garlic, pepper and sea salt over the two bowls. Add half a tablespoon of oil to both bowls. Mix well and allow to marinate for 1 hour.

Soak the rice vermicelli in warm water for 15 minutes. Remove from the water and boil for 1 minute. Drain.

Roll the diced pork belly into small balls. Fry the balls and slices of pork in the remaining oil.

Serve the meat with the rice vermicelli, herb salad and fish sauce vinaigrette.

You can also cook the meat on the barbecue or in the oven (200° C - 10 minutes).

TOM CHIEN COM DEP

CRISPY SCAMPI

12 scampi
6 tbsp flat rice flakes
(Com dep) or panko
1 egg, lightly beaten
1 tsp black sesame seeds
2 tbsp white sesame seeds
2 tsp fish sauce
Ground black pepper

SERVE WITH

Sweet & sour sauce
Herb salad
(see basic recipe pages 178-179)

12 SNACKS
10 MINUTES

Preheat the deep fryer to 180° C.

Peel the scampi up to the tail and remove the intestinal tract. Gently press them flat.

Put the scampi in a bowl and sprinkle with fish sauce and a pinch of black pepper.

In another bowl, mix the rice flakes with the sesame seeds.

Dip the prawns in the beaten egg and coat them with the rice flakes. Make sure the scampi is completely covered with rice flakes.

Fry them for 2 to 3 minutes in the deep fryer.

Serve with the sweet & sour sauce and herb salad in separate bowls.

You can replace the scampi with chicken, tofu or even vegetables, prawns or scallops.

Flat rice flakes (Com pat) can be found in Vietnamese supermarkets. You can also use panko, breadcrumbs or dried grated coconut.

Ha Long Bay

HA LONG BAY

The photogenic Ha Long Bay is surely one of the most famous spots in Vietnam: thousands of limestone islands scattered over one thousand five hundred square kilometres of crystal clear water. Islands like pearls in the sea.

Ha Long Bay is one of the most scenic areas in Vietnam. Many of the islands - of which only fifteen are inhabited - have jagged and bizarre shapes. Some look like the head of an elephant, others like fighting cocks or sleeping turtles. Some islands are hollow, with enormous caves full of stalagmites and stalactites. Others are completely covered in vegetation and are home to spectacular flora and fauna. If you slide silently on a kayak through the waters of one of the bays, you will quickly see why Ha Long Bay has been designated a UNESCO World Heritage Site and is regarded as one of the new seven wonders of the world.

HA LONG, THE DESCENDING DRAGON

This beautiful bay owes its name to an old Vietnamese legend. Whenever a neighbouring country tried to conquer Vietnam, the gods sent help in the form of a mother dragon and her children. To stop enemy boats, the dragons spat pieces of jade that turned into wondrous islands and karst mountains, thereby sinking the ships of the enemies and saving Vietnam. Since then dragons have been considered sacred in Vietnam.

"I REMEMBER THE FOOD ON THE BOAT VERY WELL. WE CAUGHT FRESH SQUID OURSELVES, WHICH WAS THEN GRILLED AND SERVED ON THE DECK. WHEN I THINK OF IT NOW MY MOUTH STILL WATERS."

"Between the islands of Ha Long Bay are floating fishing villages. The villages consist of very simple houses on wooden platforms that float on plastic barrels.
The Vietnamese families who live here live off their small fish farms and sea fishing. Some don't set foot on land for their entire lives.
The villages are well hidden among the mountains, which keeps the cottages safe from the annual typhoons."

TOM CANG NUONG

LANGOUSTINES GRILLED ON CHARCOAL

12 langoustines
1 stalk of spring onion,
finely chopped
4 garlic cloves, crushed
1 tbsp fresh ginger, grated
2 tbsp fish sauce
1 tbsp vegetable oil
2 tbsp turmeric powder
Ground black pepper and sea salt

SERVE WITH

Fish sauce vinaigrette
Herb salad
(see basic recipe pages 178-179)

SERVES 4
15 MINUTES

Make a mixture of garlic, spring onion, turmeric, ginger, oil, fish sauce, pepper and sea salt.

Halve the langoustines without peeling them and season with pepper and sea salt. Cover them with the spice mixture.

Briefly grill the langoustines on both sides on the barbecue.

Add half a teaspoon of finely chopped lemongrass, ginger and spring onion to the fish sauce vinaigrette for extra flavour.

You can also fry the langoustines in a pan with a tablespoon of oil.

MUC NUONG

FRIED SQUID

200 g squid
1 stalk of lemongrass,
finely chopped
1 stalk of spring onion,
finely chopped
2 garlic cloves, crushed
2 tbsp fresh ginger, julienned
1 tbsp fish sauce
1 tbsp vegetable oil
2 tbsp coriander, chopped
1 tsp turmeric powder
½ tsp five-spice powder
½ tsp brown sugar
Ground black pepper and sea salt

SERVES 2
15 MINUTES

Cut the squid in half and gently press flat. Make incisions and then cut into cubes.

Season the raw squid with garlic, lemongrass, fish sauce, sugar, turmeric powder, five-spice powder and pepper.

Fry the squid in oil.

Serve with coriander, fresh ginger and spring onion.

You can also grill the squid in the oven or on the barbecue. Mix one tablespoon of oil into the seasoning mix.

SO DIEP NUONG

SCALLOPS

12 scallops

3 stalks of spring onion,
finely chopped
(white and green separated)

2 garlic cloves, crushed

1 tbsp fresh ginger, grated

2 tbsp light soy sauce

1 tbsp vegetable oil

2 tbsp spring onion oil
(see basic recipe pages 178-179)

FOR 12 SERVINGS
10 MINUTES

Fry the garlic and the white part of the spring onion in oil. Fry the scallops briefly on both sides and remove from the pan.

In the same pan, fry the green part of spring onion with the ginger, soy sauce and 2 tablespoons of spring onion oil. Bring to a boil and turn off the heat.

Arrange the scallops on a plate and drizzle over the sauce.

You can garnish the scallops with julienned chilli pepper and extra ginger.

Ninh Binh

NINH BINH

Beautiful limestone mountains in a setting of narrow, winding rivers and endless paddy fields. Ninh Binh, a hidden gem and only a stone's throw from Hanoi, is an ode to nature and rural life.

There isn't much to the town itself, which makes the surrounding area all the more beautiful. The Ha Long Bay of the mainland is how Ninh Binh is often described in guidebooks. Never a truer word was spoken. Ninh Binh is easily as beautiful as Ha Long Bay. In the tenth and eleventh centuries it was home to the emperors of Vietnam. Hidden among the greenery you can find many ancient pagodas that reflect the splendour of the former empire.

Quyên: "When I first came to Ninh Binh in 2005, I was amazed by how beautiful my country was. The limestone rocks, all that green, the pagodas. We rented a boat, a red sampan, and a woman rowed us - with her feet! - into that beautiful landscape. We got to talking. I asked her if she made a living by rowing tourists across the water every day. She did not. When there were no tourists she had to go gather seaweed and snails instead. The Vietnamese are very fond of snails. Steamed. With added herbs, ginger, lime leaves, lemongrass and a fish sauce vinaigrette to make the flavour more powerful. The woman did not complain. Even though they are poor, the Vietnamese will do anything just to have good food."

"Rice is the very soul of the Vietnamese. This is obvious in Ninh Binh. Out of love for the earth on which they live and work, some farmers even build pagodas in the paddy fields so that they can be buried there. The Vietnamese eat rice every day. Sometimes they alternate: rice, rice noodles, rice paper, rice pancakes... The form does not matter, as long as it's rice (laughs)."

CANH CAI TOM BAM

SOUP OF GROUND SCAMPI AND MUSTARD LEAVES

6 scampi

200 g mustard leaves (Choi-sam) or spinach, coarsely chopped

8 stalks of spring onion, finely chopped (white and green separated)

2 garlic cloves, crushed

1 tbsp fish sauce

1 tbsp vegetable oil

1 tbsp fresh ginger, finely chopped

3 sprigs of coriander, finely chopped

Ground black pepper and sea salt

SERVES 2

15 MINUTES

Peel the scampi and remove the intestinal tract. Chop finely and mix with the green of the spring onion, half a tablespoon of fish sauce, pepper and sea salt.

Fry the garlic and the white part of the spring onion in oil. Add the scampi and stir-fry for 1 minute. Add 600 ml of water and bring to a boil, covered.

Add the mustard leaves and cook for 2 minutes. Season with the remaining fish sauce, coriander, ginger, pepper and sea salt.

You can replace the scampi with chopped eel.

VIT NUONG NGU VI

DUCK BREAST WITH FIVE-SPICE POWDER

2 duck breast fillets
1 shallot, finely chopped
2 garlic cloves, crushed
2 tbsp fresh ginger, grated
1 tbsp vegetable oil
2 tsp five-spice powder
Sea salt

FOR THE HERB MIX

Lettuce
Asian basil
Coriander
Mint
Vietnamese mint (Rau Ram)*
Shiso*

* optional

SERVE WITH

Fish sauce vinaigrette
(see basic recipe pages 178-179)

SERVES 2
20 MINUTES

Make a few incisions in the duck breast fillets and season them in a bowl with garlic, shallot, ginger, five-spice powder and a pinch of sea salt. Stir well.

Fry the duck in oil until golden brown. Make sure that the outside is crispy and the inside pink.

Cut the fillet into thin slices. Take a leaf of each herb and roll up with a slice of duck. Dip in a fish sauce vinaigrette.

You can also cook the duck in the oven (10 minutes at 200° C) or on the barbecue.

OC LUOC

COOKED SNAILS

FOR THE SNAILS

600 g snails
12 lime leaves
6 stalks of lemongrass
100 g fresh ginger,
sliced and crushed

FOR THE DIPPING SAUCE

1 tbsp lime juice
1 tsp fresh ginger, finely chopped
½ tsp garlic, finely chopped
2 lime leaves, julienned
1 tbsp fish sauce
1 tsp brown sugar

SNACK FOR 2
15 MINUTES

Soak and rinse the snails thoroughly in cold water until all the sand has been removed.

Finely chop 1 teaspoon of the white part of the lemongrass and set it aside for the dipping sauce. Leave the rest of the stalks whole and crush them.

Put the lime leaves in the bottom of a pot along with the crushed lemongrass stalks and ginger. Place the snails on top and cover with 600 ml of water. Cook for 20 minutes.

Mix the ingredients for the dipping sauce with 1 teaspoon of finely chopped lemongrass and then add 1 tablespoon of cooking liquid.

Take the snails from the pot and serve them with the dipping sauce.

GA NUONG LA CHANH

GRILLED CHICKEN WITH LIME LEAVES

4 chicken thighs, skinned
4 lime leaves, finely chopped
2 stalks of lemongrass, finely chopped
1 shallot, finely chopped
4 garlic cloves, crushed
4 tbsp fish sauce
1 tbsp vegetable oil
1 tsp five-spice powder
1 tsp turmeric powder
1 tsp brown sugar
Sea salt

SERVE WITH

Peanut sauce
(see basic recipe pages 178-179)

SERVES 4
20 MINUTES

Season the chicken thighs in a bowl with lime leaves, five-spice powder, lemongrass, fish sauce, garlic, sugar, turmeric, shallots and a pinch of sea salt. You can let the chicken marinate for several hours or use it immediately.

Fry the chicken in oil on both sides until cooked.

Cut the chicken into strips and serve with warm peanut sauce.

You can also cook the chicken in the oven (15 minutes at 200° C) or on the barbecue.

You can serve this dish with rice, herb salad and cucumber.

Hue

HUE

Hue was the imperial capital of Vietnam for many years. And you can still see and feel this fact in everything. On the streets and also in the kitchen. Hue is still the city with the most exquisite gastronomy in the country.

Hue is located on the banks of the Perfume River in the middle of Vietnam. It is a busy place, with cars and scooters constantly crisscrossing the city. But there are many architectural gems to be discovered. The Citadel, for instance, where you will find the Civil City, the Imperial City and the Hidden Purple City. An elegant complex of temples, palaces, ramparts, bastions and canals dating back to the early nineteenth century. And then there are the seven imperial tombs scattered around the south of the city. For fans of rich cultural heritage Hue represents the very best that Vietnam has to offer.

Quyên: "Hue is very special to me. Even though the last emperor was expelled in 1945 by the communist regime of Ho Chi Minh, you can still feel that imperial grandeur. When you ride along the Citadel in a bicycle rickshaw it is like taking a trip back in time. I love visiting the place. Also because I can learn a lot from the old imperial culinary traditions that are still passed on from family to family."

"There were simple snacks and real delicacies like shark fin soup or swallow's nests. There were dishes with meat or fish, but also vegetarian ones brought in by the Buddhist monks who were invited by the emperor to his palace. There was an herbalist who saw to it that every dish also had medicinal properties so that the emperor got enough vitamins and minerals to help him stay healthy. All the ingredients were carefully selected and combined. Everything had its place and function. Yin and Yang at its very best. We still reap the benefits of the basic principles that were set down back then."

"In the past the emperors were given culinary treats on a daily basis. People came from everywhere bringing the very best ingredients. The emperor ate up to sixty different dishes per meal, though only one bite of each, of course, and always the best bits. The emperor's wives - he had many, sometimes one hundred and thirty! - competed to offer him the best dish in the hope that he would visit them at night."

BUN BO HUE

BROTH OF BEEF SHANK AND LEMONGRASS

400 g ham

400 g beef shank or bouilli

120 g beef or roast beef,
in thin slices

200 g thick rice noodles
(Bun bo hue)

6 stalks of lemongrass,
crushed and halved

1 stalk of lemongrass,
finely chopped

1 onion, coarsely chopped

1 shallot, in rings

5 white stalks of
spring onion, crushed

4 cm fresh ginger, crushed

3 tbsp fish sauce

1 tbsp vegetable oil

2 cinnamon sticks

1 tsp paprika

1 tbsp brown sugar

2 tsp fish sauce

SERVE WITH

Herb salad
(see basic recipe pages 178-179)

SERVES 4
90 MINUTES
+ 2 HOURS SOAKING

Soak the rice noodles in warm water for 2 hours. Remove from the water and cook until tender. Drain.

Soak the ham and beef shank for 5 minutes in boiling salted water. Pour the meat into a colander and rinse with water.

Bring 3 litres of water to the boil and add the meat. Leave to cook for 1 hour over a low heat and remove the froth at regular intervals.

Add the lemongrass stalks, ginger, cinnamon sticks and onion and continue to cook until the meat is tender.

When the meat is cooked add the spring onion stalks and season to taste with fish sauce, sugar and sea salt. Cook for another 10 minutes.

In the meantime, fry the shallot and the finely chopped lemongrass in oil. Remove from the heat and stir in the paprika powder until the oil turns orange. Add to the soup.

Remove the ham and beef shank from the soup and cut into very thin slices.

Divide the rice noodles over four soup bowls. Place the sliced ham and beef shank and the slices of raw beef on top. Pour in the hot broth so that the raw beef can continue to cook. Garnish with some herb salad.

Bun bo hue noodles are sold in Asian supermarkets. You can also use other rice noodles.

"My son Kenny's favourite!"

DAU HU KHO NAM

STEW OF TOFU WITH RED RICE AND VEGETABLES

FOR THE STEW

200 g tofu
8 button or shiitake mushrooms, quartered
1 onion, finely chopped
1 shallot, finely chopped
2 tbsp fresh ginger, finely chopped
2 tbsp dark soy sauce
2 tbsp vegetable oil
½ tsp brown sugar
Sea salt

FOR THE MORNING GLORY (WATER SPINACH)

400 g morning glory, coarsely chopped
1 tsp garlic, crushed
1 tbsp light soy sauce
1 tbsp vegetable oil

FOR THE RICE

50 g red rice
50 g whole grain rice

SERVES 2
60 MINUTES
+ A FEW HOURS SOAKING

THE RICE

Soak the two types of rice together for a few hours in cold water. Drain and wash the rice with your hands.

Cook the rice in twice the amount of water and reduce the heat when it reaches boiling point. Cover and leave to cook over a low heat until all the liquid has been absorbed.

THE STEW

Cut the tofu into cubes and fry in 1 tablespoon of oil until golden brown.

Sauté the onion and shallot in the remaining oil. Add the mushrooms and 100 ml of water. Add the fried tofu and season with ginger, soy sauce, sugar and a pinch of sea salt.

THE MORNING GLORY (WATER SPINACH)

Fry the garlic in oil. Add the morning glory and then add a little water. Cover and leave to stew gently. Season with soy sauce.

Serve the stew with red rice and the stewed morning glory.

You can replace morning glory with other vegetables (broccoli, cauliflower, endive, Chinese cabbage, spinach...).

Sprinkle some toasted sesame seeds on the red rice for extra flavour.

BUN XAO NGHE

FRIED RICE NOODLES WITH VEGETABLES

100 g rice noodles
50 g bean sprouts
1 small leek, julienned
4 button mushrooms, sliced
¼ red bell pepper, cut into strips
3 stalks of spring onion,
finely chopped
(white and green separated)
1 tbsp fish sauce
1 tbsp light soy sauce
1 tbsp vegetable oil
1 tbsp roasted sesame seeds
or cashews, pine nuts...
1 tsp turmeric powder
Ground black pepper and sea salt

SERVES 1
15 MINUTES

Soak the rice noodles in warm water for 2 hours until soft. Drain.

Sauté the white part of the spring onion in oil. Add the leeks, mushrooms and red bell pepper and fry.

Add the noodles and fry until done. Season with the fish sauce, soy sauce and turmeric. Stir in the bean sprouts and season with pepper and sea salt.

Finally, add the green part of the spring onion and stir one last time. Garnish with toasted sesame seeds.

Choose whatever vegetables you like to eat.

You can also add strips of fried tofu to the dish.

GOI BUOI

PINK GRAPEFRUIT SALAD WITH SCAMPI

8 scampi

2 pink grapefruit, cut into wedges

1 onion, in thin rings

1 chilli pepper, finely chopped

½ lime

2 tbsp fish sauce vinaigrette
(see basic recipe pages 178-179)

1 tbsp unsalted, roasted peanuts,
finely chopped

8 mint leaves, finely chopped

2 Vietnamese mint leaves
(rau ram)*

* optional

SERVES 2
15 MINUTES

Slice open the backs of the scampi and remove the intestinal tract. Boil them in water, peel and halve them.

Mix the scampi with the grapefruit wedges, onion rings, chilli pepper and mint in a bowl.

Sprinkle the grapefruit salad with 2 tablespoons of fish sauce vinaigrette and squeeze the juice of half a lime on top. Stir gently.

Garnish with roasted peanuts and a Vietnamese mint leaf *.

You can replace the grapefruit with julienned chicory or cabbage and the scampi with chicken or other meat.

CANH DAU HU

SOUP WITH TOFU AND TOMATO

250 g tofu, cubed
2 tomatoes, finely chopped
4 cherry tomatoes, halved
1 shallot, finely chopped
1 stalk of spring onion,
finely chopped
1 garlic clove, crushed
2 tbsp fish sauce
1 tbsp vegetable oil
Brown sugar
1 tbsp coriander, finely chopped
Ground black pepper and sea salt

SERVES 2
15 MINUTES

Sauté the shallot and garlic in oil. Add the tomatoes and leave to simmer until they begin to lose their colour. Add 750 ml of water.

Once the soup is boiling, add the tofu and the cherry tomatoes. Season with fish sauce, a pinch of brown sugar and pepper and sea salt.

Allow to cook for a few minutes and then remove from the heat. Garnish with spring onion and coriander.

In Vietnam, soup is always eaten with boiled rice.

DAU HU SOT TUONG

DEEP-FRIED TOFU WITH SOY-LEMON DRESSING

250 g tofu, in large slices

SOY SAUCE & LEMONGRASS
DRESSING

1 tbsp lemongrass, finely chopped
1 tbsp spring onion,
finely chopped
1 tbsp lime juice
1 tbsp light soy sauce
1 tsp sesame oil

SNACK FOR 2
10 MINUTES

Preheat the deep fryer to 180° C.

Deep-fry the tofu slices for 2 to 3 minutes. Allow to drain on kitchen paper. Cut into small, bite-sized cubes.

Mix the lime vinaigrette with the soy sauce and lemongrass. Garnish with the spring onion and sesame oil.

Dip the tofu cubes in the vinaigrette.

This dish can be served as a snack or as a full meal with rice, stir-fried vegetables and roasted, unsalted cashew nuts or sunflower seeds, pistachio nuts...

GOI CUON CHAY

SPRING ROLLS WITH TOFU AND VEGETABLES

40 g tofu
2 tbsp soybean vermicelli
10 rice sheets
10 lettuce leaves
10 sprigs of coriander
10 mint leaves
1 stalk of lemongrass,
finely chopped
1 small onion, finely chopped
1 carrot
1 small leek
2 stalks of spring onion
4 button mushrooms
2 tbsp vegetable oil
2 tsp toasted sesame seeds
½ tsp sea salt

SERVE WITH

Soy dipping sauce
(see basic recipe pages 178-179)

SERVES 2
20 MINUTES

Soak the soybean vermicelli in hot water for 5 minutes, drain and cut into short pieces.

Cut the tofu, carrot, leek, spring onion and mushrooms into julienne strips.

Fry the tofu in 1 tablespoon of oil until golden brown.

Heat the remaining oil in a pan and fry the onion, leek and carrot. Stir and then add the mushrooms. Cover and leave to simmer until the vegetables are tender.

Add the soybean vermicelli, tofu and spring onion to the vegetables and season with sea salt. Remove from the heat, but keep warm.

Dip the rice sheets one by one very briefly in hot water until soft. Place them on a damp towel.

Divide the lettuce, coriander and mint over the rice sheets and place some of the fried tofu mixture on top. Sprinkle with toasted sesame seeds and roll up.

Add 1 teaspoon of finely chopped lemongrass to the soy dipping sauce and serve with the spring rolls.

You can use whatever you like in the rolls: fish, scampi, meat...

CA RI RAU CU

MIXED VEGETABLES IN CURRY SAUCE

2 carrots, coarsely chopped

2 sweet potatoes, coarsely chopped

20 green beans, halved

1 onion, coarsely chopped

2 stalks of lemongrass crushed and coarsely chopped

1 stalk of lemongrass, finely chopped

4 sprigs of coriander

2 tsp red curry paste

100 ml coconut milk

2 tbsp fish sauce

2 tbsp vegetable oil

Brown sugar

1 tsp turmeric powder

Sea salt

SERVES 4

30 MINUTES

Sauté the coarsely chopped lemongrass stalks in oil. Add the carrot, finely chopped lemongrass, onion and curry paste. Add 600 ml of water and leave to simmer for 10 minutes. Add the sweet potatoes and green beans.

When the vegetables are cooked add the coconut milk, fish sauce, a pinch of brown sugar and sea salt. Stir well and leave to stew for 1 minute.

Garnish with coriander leaves.

You can replace the red curry paste with yellow curry paste for a less spicy flavour.

You can serve this dish with French bread or white rice sprinkled with spring onion and black sesame seeds.

Hoi
An

HOI AN

Beautiful historic buildings, ornately decorated houses and large Chinese lanterns enhance the streets of Hoi An. No wonder that almost the entire city is included on Unesco's World Heritage List.

Hoi An is a little like Bruges. Picturesque, rich in history and, above all, boasting a magnificent display of architecture. Because of the city's location on the coast, in the sixteenth and seventeenth centuries it was an important port where ships from all over the world came to unload their cargo. Silk and spices were particularly valuable commodities. This foreign trade also brought many outside influences that are still visible in the city. The beautiful ancient Chinese trading houses and the Japanese bridge in particular steal the show.

In the evening the lights are extinguished in Hoi An. Only the colourful lanterns are left burning, creating a fairytale-like spectacle. Hoi An then becomes a magical city where tourists can offer candles to the river and cute little girls go about selling homemade lanterns.

Quyên: "The magical atmosphere of Hoi An always reminds me of my childhood. My grandparents did not have electricity in their house. When it got dark we had to make do with oil lamps. At home we did have electricity, but that often went out. So even there I often had to burn oil lamps. When all the lights go off in Hoi An, and lanterns are the only source of light, I feel like that little girl of yesteryear again."

"HERBS ARE IMMENSELY IMPORTANT IN VIETNAMESE CUISINE. NO VIETNAMESE DISH IS COMPLETE WITHOUT A BUNDLE OF HERBS. THEY PROVIDE THE EXTRA TOUCH AND THE NECESSARY NUTRITIONAL BALANCE."

"An ecological herb village was created in Hoi An a few years ago. Tra Que. Two hundred and twenty families of farmers plant fresh herbs there for the whole country: mint, coriander, spring onion, shiso, basil... Everything is organic. Instead of fertilizer, the farmers use seaweed fished from the river in Hoi An. It is a tradition that has existed for hundreds of years."

CANH MUOP NHOI THIT GA

STUFFED COURGETTE WITH CHICKEN AND VEGETABLES

1 courgette

100 g chicken

2 tbsp soybean vermicelli

2 shiitake mushrooms
or mushrooms, finely chopped

3 stalks of spring onion,
finely chopped
(white and green separated)

1 shallot, finely chopped

3 sprigs of coriander,
roughly chopped

1 tbsp fish sauce

1 tbsp vegetable oil

Ground black pepper and sea salt

SERVES 2
20 MINUTES

Soak the soybean vermicelli in hot water for 5 minutes, drain and cut into short pieces.

Cut the courgette into 3 cm slices and remove the seeds.

In a bowl mix the chicken with half of the fish sauce, the white part of the spring onions, the shiitake mushrooms and the soybean vermicelli. Season with sea salt.

Grind together and use the mix to stuff the courgette slices.

Sauté the shallot in oil. After 1 minute, add 600 ml of water and bring to the boil. Place the stuffed courgette slices in the soup and cook for 5 minutes. Season with sea salt and the remaining fish sauce. Remove from the heat.

Pour the soup into two bowls and garnish with the green part of the spring onion, coriander and pepper.

BANH XEO

PANCAKE WITH SCAMPI AND PORK BELLY

FOR THE BATTER

200 g rice flour or Banh Xeo flour

4 stalks of spring onion (green), finely chopped

2 tsp turmeric powder

FOR THE STUFFING

100 g pork belly, in thin slices

8 prawns, peeled and halved lengthwise

1 handful of bean sprouts

1 onion, in rings

1 shallot, finely chopped

4 stalks of spring onion (white), finely chopped

2 tsp fish sauce

1 tbsp vegetable oil

Ground black pepper and sea salt

SERVE WITH

Fish sauce vinaigrette

Herb salad

(see basic recipe pages 178-179)

SERVES 2
20 MINUTES

Make the pancake batter with the rice flour and 300 ml of water. Add the green part of the spring onion and the turmeric.

Place the bacon along with the prawns in a bowl and add the shallots, the white part of the spring onion and the fish sauce. Season with salt and pepper and stir.

Heat the oil in a frying pan and sauté half of the onion rings. Add half of the bacon and sauté briefly. Add 4 of the prawns, turn after 1 minute and immediately pour in another spoonful of the batter. Cook for another 2 minutes, covered. Sprinkle over half of the bean sprouts, cover again and cook briefly. Repeat for the second pancake.

Place the pancake on a plate, fold over and serve with the fish sauce vinaigrette and herb salad on the side.

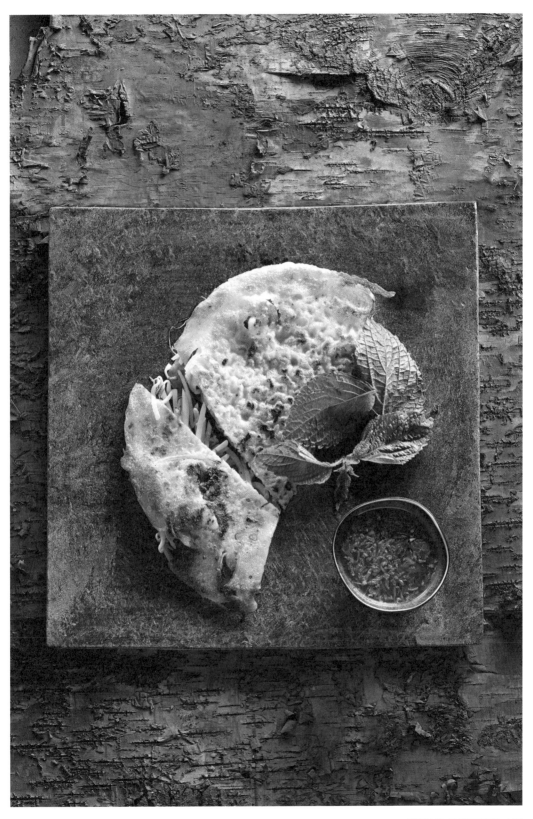

HOANH THANH TOM
SCAMPI WONTON WITH SOY DIPPING SAUCE

12 scampi
12 wonton sheets
1 shallot, finely chopped
4 stalks of spring onion,
finely chopped
(white and green separated)
1 small carrot, finely chopped
4 shiitake mushrooms or
button mushrooms, finely
chopped
1 garlic clove, crushed
1 handful of bean sprouts
1 egg, lightly beaten
1 tbsp fish sauce
Ground black pepper

SERVE WITH

Soy dipping sauce
(see basic recipe pages 178-179)

SERVES 2
15 MINUTES

Peel the scampi and remove the intestinal tract. Mix them together with the shallot and white part of the spring onion in a food processor.

Put the finely ground scampi in a bowl and season with fish sauce, garlic and pepper. Add the shiitake mushrooms, the green of the spring onion and the carrot and stir.

Brush the edges of the wonton sheets with the beaten egg and add 1 teaspoon of stuffing to each sheet. Fold into the desired shape.

Place a few bean sprouts in the steamer basket so that the wontons do not stick to the bottom. Steam for 5 minutes.

Serve with soy dipping sauce.

You can also fill the wontons with ground pork belly.

You can also deep-fry the wontons (3 to 4 minutes at 180° C). Serve with sweet & sour sauce and herb salad (see basic recipe pages 178-179).

GA XAO GUNG

MECHELEN COUCOU WITH GINGER

160 g Mechelen Coucou (chicken) fillet, in cubes
1 tbsp fresh ginger, grated
1 tbsp fresh ginger, julienned
1 tbsp fish sauce
1 tbsp light soy sauce
1 tbsp vegetable oil
1 tsp brown sugar

SERVES 2
10 MINUTES

Heat the oil with the sugar in a saucepan over a medium heat and allow to caramelize. Add the grated ginger and fry the coucou fillet.

Once the coucou is tender, add the fish sauce and soy sauce. Stir-fry for 1 minute and remove from the heat.

Garnish with julienned ginger.

You can serve this dish with rice and stir-fried vegetables.

CHA TOM CHIEN

OMELETTE WITH SCAMPI

4 eggs

6 scampi, peeled and
finely chopped

2 tbsp soybean vermicelli

1 shallot, finely chopped

4 stalks of spring onion,
finely chopped
(white and green separated)

2 garlic cloves, crushed

1 tsp fresh ginger, grated

1 tbsp light soy sauce

1 tbsp fish sauce

1 tbsp vegetable oil

Ground black pepper and sea salt

SERVES 2

10 MINUTES

Soak the soybean vermicelli in hot water for 5 minutes, drain and cut into short strips.

Beat the eggs in a bowl with the green part of the spring onion, soybean vermicelli, fish sauce and soy sauce.

Season the scampi with the shallots, garlic, ginger, pepper and sea salt. Stir well.

Heat the oil in a pan and sauté the white part of the spring onion. Add the scampi and sauté gently. Pour in the egg mixture and fry until done.

You can replace the scampi with chopped pork belly.

Quy
Nhon

QUY NHON

Quy Nhon is a coastal town in the middle of Vietnam with long, white beaches. Quyên was born here fourteen years before she came to Belgium. She does not have particularly great memories of the place: "It was hard work every day." But now, many years later, she can appreciate its beauty.

A GIANT TUNA

Quyên: "Fishing is very important in Quy Nhon. It always has been. As a child I ate fish almost every day. When my father was still living with us in Vietnam I often went fishing with him on the beach. I sat next to him waiting for the fish to bite. Sometimes I got to do some fishing myself. He taught me how to watch the rod and what to do if it moved. Fishing is very relaxing. And when the fish bites you feel elated. One day we caught a giant tuna. It was so heavy that it almost broke my father's small fishing rod. What a commotion! And what a fish! My father sold the tuna at the market and for the next few days we had food in abundance."

"As a girl I was never allowed to join my father on his fishing boat. That is a Vietnamese tradition: girls or women on a boat bring misfortune. My brothers were all allowed to go along. I never questioned it. That was just the way it was. I sometimes swam into the sea and held on to my dad's boat so that I could peek over the edge. But that was as far as I got."

"Now there are almost no fish left near the coast of Quy Nhon, but at that time my father could still catch plenty of fish. Back then it was sold right there on the beach. Sometimes I was given a few fish to sell. I'd go off to the market, set up a stall and try to sell the fish. I was good at it. Even though I was no older than eight or nine at the time. My cousins asked me to sell their fish as well, because boys were not allowed to enter the market. They kept a close eye on me to make sure I didn't keep the money for myself. Which I obviously didn't do. I did receive a small commission, however. I was an entrepreneur from a very young age, I guess (laughs)."

"ONE DAY WE CAUGHT A GIANT TUNA. IT WAS SO HEAVY THAT IT ALMOST BROKE MY FATHER'S SMALL FISHING ROD. WHAT A COMMOTION! AND WHAT A FISH! MY FATHER SOLD THE TUNA AT THE MARKET AND FOR THE NEXT FEW DAYS WE HAD FOOD IN ABUNDANCE."

"My village has changed beyond recognition. When I returned for the first time twelve years ago I recognised almost nothing. My old house was gone. All the roads had been paved and the houses looked very different. There is less poverty, though many Vietnamese still have to work very hard to make ends meet. Two hundred thousand people live there now. How many were there back in my day? I have no idea. I knew only one street. And the people at the market and in the fishing village."

CHAO BO CAU

RICE SOUP WITH PIGEON AND MUNG BEANS

1 pigeon
6 tbsp washed rice
3 tbsp soaked mung beans, peeled
(available at Asian grocery stores)
1 onion, quartered
3 stalks of spring onion
(white and green separated)
4 tbsp fish sauce
Ground black pepper and sea salt

SERVES 2
45 MINUTES

Bring 3 litres of water to the boil. Add the pigeon together with the onion, rice and mung beans. Leave to simmer partially covered for 1 hour on a low heat.

Crush the white part of the spring onion and add it to the pot. Cook for another 10 minutes. Season with fish sauce and pepper.

Scoop the pigeon out of the pot. Remove the meat and put it back in the pot. Stir gently.

Serve with the finely chopped green of the spring onion.

You can replace the mung beans with lotus seeds.

NGHEU NUONG MO HANH
GRILLED COCKLES

20 cockles
1 chilli pepper, finely chopped
3 tbsp unsalted, roasted peanuts, finely chopped
2 tbsp fish sauce

SERVE WITH

Fish sauce vinaigrette
Spring onion oil
(see basic recipe pages 178-179)

SERVES 2
10 MINUTES

Preheat the oven to 200° C.

Rinse the cockles with water. Open them a little and fill with fish sauce and the finely chopped chilli pepper.

Grill the cockles in the oven for 3 minutes.

Open them fully and spoon over the fish sauce vinaigrette and spring onion oil. Garnish with roasted peanuts.

RECIPE BY MY SISTER HOA
Vietnamese restaurant Bun - Antwerp

Very tasty when cooked in a charcoal oven or on the bbq.

DAU QUE XAO BO

GREEN BEANS WITH BEEF AND TOMATO

100 g beef, in thin slices
300 g green beans
8 cherry tomatoes, halved
1 onion, in half rings
4 garlic cloves, crushed
1 tbsp fish sauce
1 tsp dark soy sauce
2 tbsp vegetable oil
4 sprigs of coriander,
roughly chopped
Ground black pepper and sea salt

SERVES 2
15 MINUTES

Rinse the beans, cut the ends off and halve them.

Sauté the garlic and beans in 1 tablespoon of oil. Add 100 ml of water and cook for 5 minutes, covered. Stir frequently. Season with sea salt and spoon onto a plate.

Gently sauté the tomatoes and onion in the remaining oil until soft. Add the meat and the cooked beans. Season with fish sauce and soy sauce and stir. Remove from the heat so that the meat will remain pink in the middle. Season with pepper and coriander.

Serve with rice.

CA CHEM HAP

STEAMED SEA BASS

1 sea bass (600 g)
2 tbsp soybean vermicelli
¼ pineapple, diced
4 okra or green beans,
halved lengthwise*
4 shiitake mushrooms
or chanterelles, chopped
½ red bell pepper, julienned
1 small carrot, julienned
2 stalks of spring onion,
finely chopped
1 shallot, finely chopped
1 tbsp fresh ginger, julienned
1 tbsp vegetable oil
1 tbsp light soy sauce
Ground black pepper

FOR THE MARINADE

1 shallot, finely chopped
1 tbsp fresh ginger, finely chopped
1 tbsp fish sauce
1 tbsp vegetable oil
Ground black pepper and sea salt

* optional

SERVES 2
20 MINUTES

Soak the soybean vermicelli in hot water for 5 minutes, drain and cut into short strips.

Make three deep incisions on either side of the sea bass and loosen the gills.

Mix the ingredients for the marinade. Fill the incisions and the gills with the mixture. Steam the fish for 10 minutes and retain the cooking juices.

Sauté the shallots, ginger and spring onion in oil. Add the carrot, red bell pepper, shiitake mushrooms and okra and sauté, stirring continuously.

Finally, mix in the soybean vermicelli and pineapple, fry for 1 more minute and season with 2 tablespoons of the cooking juices, soy sauce and pepper.

Serve the fish on a large plate and with the fried vegetables.

Make this dish with whatever vegetables you like.

BI DO XAO TOM

PUMPKIN WITH SCAMPI

12 scampi

1 small pumpkin, peeled and cut into thin slices (200 g)

1 shallot, finely chopped

2 stalks of spring onion, finely chopped

2 garlic cloves, crushed

2 tbsp fish sauce

1 tbsp vegetable oil

40 Asian basil leaves, or coriander, spring onion...

Ground black pepper and sea salt

SERVES 2
20 MINUTES

Peel the scampi and remove the intestinal tract. Crush them lightly with the flat side of a knife and chop finely. Marinate in 1 tablespoon of fish sauce, the spring onion, 1 clove of crushed garlic, pepper and sea salt.

Sauté the rest of the garlic and shallot in oil. Add the chopped scampi and stir well to ensure that they do not stick.

When the scampi are almost done, add the pumpkin. Pour in the rest of the fish sauce and 200 ml of water. Leave to simmer for 5 minutes, covered and on a medium heat. Stir frequently.

Garnish with Asian basil.

You can replace the scampi with chopped pork belly or with chopped pistachios for a vegetarian option.

Excellent with Hokkaido pumpkin (Japanese pumpkin).

QUY NHON . BI DO XAO TOM . 127

CHA CA QUY NHON

QUY NHON FISHCAKES

300 g red mullet fillet or other
firm fish, such as sole, cod...

5 stalks of spring onion,
finely chopped
(white and green separated)

3 garlic cloves, crushed

1 tbsp fish sauce

1 tsp sesame oil

1 tbsp vegetable oil

Sea salt

SERVE WITH

Fish sauce vinaigrette
Herb salad
(see basic recipe pages 178-179)

FOR 12 CAKES
30 MINUTES

Crumble the fish finely and place in a bowl. Season with garlic, fish sauce, sesame oil, the white of the spring onion and a pinch of sea salt. Stir well and make small balls from the mixture.

Flatten the balls and fry until golden brown on both sides.

Serve on a plate garnished with the green of the spring onion, fish sauce vinaigrette and herb salad.

You can also serve the fish cakes with noodle soup.

SU SU XAO TRUNG

CHAYOTE WITH EGGS

2 su su (chayote) or cucumbers,
peeled and sliced

2 eggs, lightly beaten

2 stalks of spring onion,
finely chopped
(white and green separated)

3 garlic cloves, crushed

1 tbsp fish sauce

1 tbsp vegetable oil

2 sprigs of coriander,
roughly chopped

Ground black pepper and sea salt

SERVES 2
15 MINUTES

Stir-fry the garlic in oil along with the white part of the spring onion and the su su. Then add 100 ml of water. Leave to simmer for 3 minutes, covered and on a medium heat.

When the su su is done add the eggs. Season with fish sauce, the green part of the spring onion, coriander, pepper and sea salt. Stir and serve.

DAU HU CHIEN SA

TOFU WITH LEMONGRASS

1 block tofu (± 300 g)

2 stalks of lemongrass, finely chopped (+ extra for garnish)

3 stalks of spring onion, finely chopped

1 chilli pepper, finely chopped

3 garlic cloves, crushed

2 tbsp light soy sauce

1 tbsp vegetable oil

2 sprigs of coriander, roughly chopped

Sea salt

SERVES 2
15 MINUTES

Wash the tofu and pat dry with kitchen paper. Cut into small bite-sized cubes.

Mix the spring onions, lemongrass, garlic, chilli pepper, soy sauce and a pinch of sea salt in a bowl. Brush the tofu cubes with this mixture on both sides.

Fry the tofu in oil until golden brown. Arrange them on a plate and garnish with coriander and some extra lemongrass if you like.

You can serve this dish with rice and roasted cashews.

SU SU

"Like all Vietnamese abroad, my father also has his own vegetable garden here in Belgium. He grows organic herbs there for my restaurant and also chayote or susu, an Asian vegetable that resembles a pear, with light green flesh and a taste similar to cucumber. We use it mainly in soups and stir-fries."

Ho Chi
Minh City

HO CHI MINH CITY

Pedicab drivers resting under huge neon signs, the Vietnamese middle class driving around on imported motorcycles in haute couture clothing, an old woman selling noodles from her mobile stall. Welcome to Ho Chi Minh City, a glorious mix of colour, aroma and hustle and bustle!

Ho Chi Minh City, formerly known as Saigon, is the largest city in Vietnam.

From 1955 to 1975 it was the capital of what was then the independent republic of South Vietnam. South Vietnam was capitalist and anti-communist and fought against the communist North Vietnam and the Viet Cong during the Vietnam War, in which it was supported by the United States, among others. In 1975, however, Saigon was conquered by the communists and the city was renamed Ho Chi Minh City, in honour of the leader of the Communists, Ho Chi Minh. The name Saigon is still used by many today.

THE GREAT CROSSING

Quyên: "Saigon will always remind me of our journey to Belgium in 1986. We took the night train from my home town of Quy Nhon to Saigon. This was quite an experience because the train was packed with people, chickens and ducks. We slept among them on the ground. The plan was to take the plane from Ho Chi Minh City to Belgium. But our papers were not in order and my mother had to return to our village. My siblings and I were left in Ho Chi Minh City with the friend of an uncle. I was fourteen and had never been to the big city before. But I had to make the best of it and buy groceries to cook for my brothers and sisters. I went to the market to buy fruit and vegetables. The people laughed at me because of my dialect. I felt terrible. How was I to know that people spoke differently in another part of my country? It was a huge blow to my self-confidence. Everything was so big and unfamiliar. I didn't know anyone. It made me very insecure. It took four days for my mother to return. To me it seemed like an eternity."

"HO CHI MINH IS A VIBRANT CITY WITH A WIDE RANGE OF GREAT SHOPS AND FINE FOOD. IT IS A MELTING POT OF DELICACIES WITH INFLUENCES FROM EVERYWHERE."

BO NUONG LA LOT

BEEF ROLLED IN LA LOT LEAVES

160 g beef, minced

12 wild betel (La Lot)
or Shiso leaves

100 g rice vermicelli

2 stalks of lemongrass,
finely chopped

1 shallot, finely chopped

3 stalks of spring onion,
finely chopped
(white and green separated)

3 garlic cloves, crushed

2 tsp unsalted, roasted peanuts
or cashew nuts, finely chopped

1 tbsp fish sauce

2 tbsp vegetable oil

1 tsp five-spice powder

1 tsp turmeric powder

SERVE WITH

Fish sauce vinaigrette
Spring onion oil
(see basic recipe pages 178-179)

SERVES 2
20 MINUTES

Soak the rice vermicelli in warm water for 15 minutes. Remove from the water and boil for 1 minute. Drain.

Mix the beef in a bowl with the shallots, half of the garlic, the white of the spring onion and the lemongrass. Season with fish sauce, 1 tablespoon of oil, five-spice powder and turmeric. Mix all ingredients together well.

Take the betel leaves and spread the meat mixture on the light side of the leaves. Roll them up and fasten with a skewer.

Fry the skewers in the remaining oil and garlic.

Mix 1 tablespoon of water with the fish sauce vinaigrette.

Serve with the fish sauce vinaigrette and the rice vermicelli and sprinkle with the spring onion oil. Garnish with peanuts and the green part of the spring onion.

GOI CAI XOONG BO

BEEF AND WATERCRESS SALAD

100 g beef, in slices

2 bunches of watercress

1 red onion, in rings

2 stalks of lemongrass, finely chopped

2 garlic cloves, crushed

1 tbsp unsalted, roasted peanuts, finely chopped

Fish sauce vinaigrette (see basic recipe pages 178-179)

1 tbsp fish sauce

2 tbsp vegetable oil

2 tsp white sesame seeds

Ground black pepper

SERVES 2
15 MINUTES

Season the beef slices in a bowl with 1 tablespoon of oil, fish sauce, garlic, lemongrass and pepper. Stir well.

In another bowl, mix the watercress with the red onion and divide over two plates. Sprinkle the watercress salad with fish sauce vinaigrette.

Fry the beef slices very briefly on both sides in the remaining oil, ensuring that it remains pink and juicy on the inside.

Arrange the meat on top of the watercress salad and garnish with peanuts and sesame seeds.

You can also garnish this dish with fried shallots (see basic recipe pages 178-179).

BANH MI THIT

VIETNAMESE SANDWICH

1 baguette

300 g bacon or pork, in pieces

1 carrot, grated into long, thin slices

1 small daikon radish or white turnip, grated into long, thin slices

1 cucumber in long, thin slices

1 stalk of lemongrass, finely chopped

3 tsp fish sauce

2 tbsp light soy sauce

2 tsp lime juice

4 tsp mayonnaise

4 tsp butter

1 tbsp vegetable oil

1 tsp brown sugar

1 tsp turmeric powder

1 tsp five-spice powder

Sea salt

SERVES 4
15 MINUTES

Marinate the meat in a pinch of sea salt, turmeric powder, half of the five-spice powder and half of the lemongrass. Sprinkle with 2 teaspoons of fish sauce.

Season the slices of carrot, daikon radish and cucumber in a bowl with lime juice, sugar and a pinch of sea salt. Stir well.

Fry the meat in oil along with the remaining lemongrass.

Season the meat with the rest of the fish sauce and the five-spice powder. Stir-fry until the bacon is done.

Divide the baguette into four pieces and cut in half. Spread one side with butter and the other with mayonnaise. Add the marinated slices of carrot, daikon radish and cucumber. Top off with the meat and sprinkle with soy sauce.

You can also add some spring onion and coriander to the sandwich if you like.

For a lightly spicy flavour, add chopped chilli peppers to the soy sauce.

NEM CHUOI

SWEET BANANA NEM

3 bananas

12 round rice sheets
(16 cm in diameter)

2 tsp unsalted, roasted
peanuts, finely chopped

3 tsp white sesame seeds

1 tsp black sesame seeds

400 ml coconut milk

6 tsp brown sugar

MAKES 12 SERVINGS
10 MINUTES

Cut each banana in half and then halve them lengthwise.

Soak the rice sheets very briefly in hot water until soft. Put them on a damp towel or a plate.

Place a piece of banana on each rice sheet and sprinkle with white and black sesame seeds. Spoon the sugar on top and roll up.

Fry the nems for 2 to 3 minutes in the deep fryer at 180° C. Drain on kitchen paper.

Heat the coconut milk and pour it over the nems. Garnish with roasted peanuts.

You can also use pineapple or apple instead of banana.

You can serve the nems with a scoop of vanilla ice cream.

STREET FOOD

IS STREET FOOD SAFE IN VIETNAM?

"Of course! The Vietnamese go to the market twice a day. Everything is fresh, light and healthy, and cooked on the spot. Each stall often has only one specialty. They cannot afford to make bad food. The Vietnamese take their gastronomy very seriously. Good food is their highest priority. They work very hard, but they also like spending whatever money they have on food. Especially in Ho Chi Minh City. They live in small houses, do not have much room to cook and so they usually eat on the street. Three times a day. These are not gourmet dinners with a three-course meal, like we're used to. They eat a lot of small snacks to give them enough energy to keep going. Some cook at home at night, others never do. But street food is an absolute must for tourists visiting Vietnam. It's very tasty and, above all, inexpensive. This in itself is reason enough for me to enjoy visiting Ho Chi Minh City. The delicious smells of street food hit you on every street corner."

FRENCH INFLUENCE

The influence of the French is unmistakable in many aspects of Vietnamese cuisine. The French introduced different cooking techniques, baguettes, wine, coffee, chocolate, cakes and lots of meat.

Quyên: "In the past, the Vietnamese were prohibited from eating beef by the king. Cattle and buffaloes were only for working the land. But in the nineteenth century, when the French were all eating steak, the Vietnamese were quick to convert."

Bifteck is one of the words that quickly became established. Not to mention carotte (carrot), moutarde (mustard), artichaut (artichoke), café (coffee)...

Quyên: "Yes, coffee is a relic of French colonisation. Coffee now occupies a very important place in Vietnamese social life. Coffee bars are constantly opening in Ho Chi Minh City. Men go there with their friends in the morning to drink a cup of coffee; young people drink ice coffee with condensed milk and lots of ice. Wonderfully refreshing!"

Can
Tho

CAN THO

Can Tho is located in the heart of the Mekong Delta. It is a friendly and hospitable city where activity is centered mainly on and along the Mekong River and branching canals.

Can Tho has a simple, poetic beauty. It is a delight to take a boat trip on a beautiful day along the riverbanks and to behold the spectacle of the floating markets. Traders in fully laden boats sell their wares everywhere; everything from vegetables and fresh fruit to handmade items, pots, pans and souvenirs. Each boat has a stick on board with the items sold on the boat hanging from it. This makes it possible for customers to see from a distance where they need to go. The boats are often anchored close together and compete fiercely for customers.

Quyên: "Can Tho is still very authentic. The floating market is not there for the tourists but for the Vietnamese themselves. A place where they can buy or exchange goods. If you ever go there, be sure to eat with the locals. You will receive a warm and friendly welcome. The menu always includes crispy elephant ear fish that you can roll up in rice paper and herb salad and dip in nuoc mam cham sauce. Just thinking about it makes my mouth water!"

"THE SOIL IN CAN THO IS VERY FERTILE. MANY TYPES OF RICE AND EXOTIC FRUITS ARE GROWN: JACKFRUIT, DRAGON FRUIT, PINEAPPLE, MANGO, RAMBUTAN, MANGOSTEEN... YOU NAME IT, THEY GROW IT."

Mangosteen //

CA PHEN CHIEN
RED MULLET WITH CHICORY

2 red mullets
2 heads of chicory, julienned
1 shallot, finely chopped
1 tsp fresh ginger, grated
1 tsp lemongrass, finely chopped
1 tbsp vegetable oil
2 tbsp spring onion oil
(see basic recipe pages 178-179)
4 sprigs of coriander,
roughly chopped
Ground black pepper and sea salt

SERVE WITH

Fish sauce vinaigrette
(see basic recipe pages 178-179)

SERVES 2
10 MINUTES

Clean the fish and make three incisions in each fish using a sharp knife. Season with salt and pepper.

Arrange the chopped chicory on 2 plates.

Mix the ginger and lemongrass with the fish sauce vinaigrette.

Sauté the shallot in oil, add the fish and fry. Remove the fish from the pan when done and place it on the chicory. Sprinkle with spring onion oil.

Garnish with coriander and fish sauce vinaigrette.

You can also roll the fish in rice paper with herb salad and dip it in a fish sauce vinaigrette.

CA RI VIT

DUCK WITH YELLOW CURRY

1 small duck, cut into large pieces

2 potatoes, roughly chopped

1 sweet potato, roughly chopped

2 carrots, roughly chopped

4 stalks of lemongrass, roughly chopped

6 garlic cloves, crushed

2 tbsp fish sauce

200 ml coconut milk

1 tbsp vegetable oil

1 tsp brown sugar

4 sprigs of coriander, roughly chopped

1 tbsp yellow curry powder or red curry powder (spicier)

Sea salt

FOR THE MARINADE

2 stalks of lemongrass, finely chopped

3 garlic cloves, crushed

2 stalks of spring onion, finely chopped

2 tbsp fish sauce

1 tsp sea salt

SERVES 4

90 MINUTES +

1 HOUR MARINATING TIME

Mix all the ingredients for the marinade.

Place the pieces of duck in a large bowl and pour in the marinade. Leave to marinate for 1 hour.

Briefly sauté the lemongrass stalks in oil with garlic. Add the meat and fry until golden brown. Add the potatoes and carrots. Season with yellow curry powder, 1 tablespoon of fish sauce and sea salt.

Pour in half a litre of water and bring to the boil, covered. Reduce the heat and leave to simmer for 45 minutes, covered.

After 45 minutes, when the meat is done, add the sweet potato. Cook for 15 minutes.

Add the coconut milk, the remaining fish sauce and the brown sugar. Leave to simmer for a few minutes. Garnish with coriander leaves.

You can serve this dish with rice, rice vermicelli or a baguette for dipping in the curry sauce.

You can replace the duck with chicken.

CA NUONG LA CHUOI

BRILL FILLET IN BANANA LEAF

2 brill fillets, cut into large chunks

2 tbsp soybean vermicelli

2 banana leaves
(+/- 25 cm x 15 cm:
large enough to wrap the fish in)

6 shiitake mushrooms, in slices

3 stalks of spring onion,
finely chopped
(white and green separated)

2 garlic cloves, crushed

1 tbsp fish sauce

1 tbsp sesame oil

2 sprigs of coriander,
roughly chopped

1 tsp turmeric powder

Sea salt

SERVES 2
20 MINUTES

Preheat the oven to 180° C.

Soak the soybean vermicelli in hot water for 5 minutes, drain and cut into short strips.

Season the fish in a bowl with a pinch of sea salt, fish sauce, turmeric, the white of the spring onion, garlic and sesame oil. Stir gently.

Divide the fish between the banana leaves and add the mushrooms and the soybean vermicelli. Fold up into a packet.

Place the packets side by side in a baking dish and bake in the oven for 5 to 10 minutes.

Serve the banana leaves open on a plate and garnish with coriander and the green of the spring onion.

You can also make this dish on the barbecue.

CHAO HAI SAN

MINCED SHRIMP AND SQUID ON LEMONGRASS STICK

250 g scampi
100 g squid
4 stalks of lemongrass, halved
1 tbsp fish sauce
2 tbsp vegetable oil
4 sprigs of dill, finely chopped
Ground black pepper and sea salt

SERVE WITH

Fish sauce vinaigrette or
sweet and sour sauce
Herb salad
(see basic recipe pages 178-179)

MAKES 8 PIECES
30 MINUTES

Peel the scampi and remove the intestinal tract.

Mix the scampi and squid with 1 tablespoon of oil, fish sauce, dill, a pinch of sea salt and pepper in a food processor to a fine texture.

With moist hands, make 8 balls from the mixture and squeeze them around the top of a halved lemongrass stick.

Fry the skewers in the remaining oil.

You can replace the lemongrass stalks with sugar cane stalks.

Phu
Quoc

PHU QUOC

There is no more heavenly place in Vietnam than the island of Phu Quoc. White beaches, an emerald sea, tropical fish and... great seafood.

Phu Quoc Island lies in the south of Vietnam. It's a rather controversial spot because both Cambodia and Vietnam lay claim to this little piece of paradise. It is not large, only about fifty kilometres long and twenty five kilometres across, and about six hours by boat from the mainland. The island has not yet been overrun by hordes of tourists. Those looking for peace and quiet will certainly find it here. In some of the bays the island's unspoiled nature makes you feel like you have landed on a desert island.

But Phu Quoc is more than just fabulous beaches: on the north side of the island you will find one of the densest jungles in Vietnam. The entire island is ringed by foreboding cliffs and some people refer to Phu Quoc as the island of the ninety-nine hills. But most importantly: the best fish sauce factory in South East Asia is located on Phu Quoc! Why? Quyên: "The fish sauce is made from anchovies. When the fish are caught they are immediately marinated in sea salt on the boat. The mixture always consists of seventy per cent anchovies and thirty per cent sea salt. The fish are placed in a sealed timber barrel and left to ferment for six to fifteen months. The fish and salt mix is then pressed, with the first pressing giving the very best juice. This first pressing is followed by a second pressing, which is mixed with water. The leftovers are used as fertilizer on the plantations."

"THE FISH SAUCE FROM PHU QUOC IS THE CHAMPAGNE OF FISH SAUCES: HIGH QUALITY AND VERY HEALTHY!"

"In Belgium, some people turn their noses up when I talk about fish sauce. They think it smells strange and are initially sceptical. But I always try to help them to overcome their prejudice. Because not only is fish sauce very good for flavour, it is also very healthy. Especially when you use a high quality fish sauce to which no chemical substances have been added."

TOM HUM CA RI

LOBSTER WITH YELLOW CURRY

2 lobsters (500 g/lobster)

2 tbsp soybean vermicelli

40 g young bamboo shoots, julienned

1 red bell pepper, julienned

8 mushrooms, quartered

1 courgette, sliced

1 tbsp lemongrass, finely chopped

1 shallot, finely chopped

4 stalks of spring onion, finely chopped

100 ml coconut milk

2 tbsp fish sauce

2 tbsp vegetable oil

1 tsp brown sugar

1 tbsp yellow curry powder

8 stalks Ngo om or coriander, finely chopped

Sea salt

SERVES 2

30 MINUTES

Rinse the bamboo under running water and soak for 15 minutes in hot water. Change the water regularly.

Soak the soybean vermicelli in hot water for 5 minutes, drain and cut into short strips.

Halve the lobsters lengthwise, break and crush the claws.

Sauté the spring onion, shallot and lemongrass in oil. Add the lobster and fry until it changes colour. Add the bamboo shoots, courgette, mushrooms and red bell pepper.

Add the curry powder and coconut milk to the lobster and then add 100 ml of water. Simmer for 5 minutes over a low heat.

Finally, add the fish sauce, brown sugar, soybean vermicelli and a pinch of sea salt. Cover and leave to simmer until the vegetables and lobster are tender.

Remove from the heat and garnish with Ngo om.

You can add 1 tablespoon of red curry paste for a spicier version.

GOI CA NGU
TUNA CARPACCIO

100 g tuna

1 tbsp unsalted, roasted
peanuts, finely chopped

1 shallot, in rings

½ lime, cut into wedges

1 tbsp fresh ginger, julienned

2 tbsp fish sauce vinaigrette
(see basic recipe pages 178-179)

4 leaves Vietnamese mint
(rau ram) or mint, finely chopped

4 leaves Shiso or Asian basil,
finely chopped*

* optional

SERVES 2
10 MINUTES

Pat the tuna dry and cut into very thin slices.

Arrange the tuna on 2 plates and sprinkle the shallot rings, ginger and fresh herbs on top.

Drizzle over a tablespoon of fish sauce vinaigrette and garnish with the roasted peanuts.

Serve with a wedge of lime to sprinkle on the tuna.

Briefly freeze the tuna to make it easier to cut.

You can replace the tuna with scallops or salmon.

TOM RIM

SCAMPI WITH PEPPER AND FISH SAUCE

12 scampi

2 stalks of spring onion,
finely chopped
(white and green separated)

1 garlic clove, crushed

2 tbsp fish sauce

2 sprigs of coriander,
roughly chopped

1 tbsp vegetable oil

2 tsp black peppercorns, crushed

Ground black pepper

SERVES 2
10 MINUTES

Peel the scampi up to the tail and remove the intestinal tract.

Season the scampi with fish sauce, the white part of the spring onion and black pepper. Stir well.

Sauté the garlic in the oil and add the scampi. Fry for a few minutes until done.

Finish the dish off with the green of the spring onion, coriander and black pepper.

You can serve this dish with rice or noodles and vegetables.

HEN HAP SA

MUSSELS WITH LEMONGRASS

30 mussels

1 tbsp fish sauce

6 lime leaves, crushed

2 stalks of lemongrass,
roughly cut and crushed

30 g fresh ginger,
sliced and crushed

FOR THE DIPPING SAUCE

1 wedge of lime, squeezed

Ground black pepper and sea salt

SERVES 1

15 MINUTES

Soak and rinse the mussels thoroughly in cold water until all the sand has been removed.

Heat the lemongrass with the lime leaves and ginger in a dry saucepan. Add the mussels, cover and cook for 2 to 3 minutes until all the mussels have opened.

Pour the fish sauce over the mussels, shake and turn off the heat.

Serve with a dipping sauce of sea salt, black pepper and lime juice.

NGHEU CA RI

CLAMS WITH RED CURRY

1 kg clams

4 stalks of lemongrass,
roughly chopped

4 stalks of spring onion,
finely chopped

4 garlic cloves, crushed

2 tsp galangal, crushed and sliced*

2 tsp red curry paste

6 tbsp coconut milk

2 tbsp fish sauce

1 tbsp vegetable oil

1 tsp turmeric powder

4 sprigs of coriander,
stalks and leaves separated

Sea salt

* optional

SERVES 2
10 MINUTES

Soak and rinse the clams thoroughly in cold water until all the sand has been removed.

Sauté the garlic with lemongrass and galangal in oil. Stir in the red curry paste and turmeric.

Add the clams together with 4 tablespoons of water, the coriander stalks and coconut milk. Cook until all the shells have opened. Season with fish sauce and sea salt, shake and turn off the heat.

Garnish with coriander leaves.

FISH SAUCE VINAIGRETTE
(NUOC MAM CHAM)
2 tbsp brown sugar • 4 tbsp lime juice •
4 tbsp fish sauce • 1 tsp chilli pepper,
finely chopped • 2 garlic cloves,
crushed and finely chopped

With chilli peppers for the spicy food enthusiast.

SOY DIPPING SAUCE
(SOT TUONG GUNG)
1 tbsp brown sugar • 2 tbsp lime juice •
2 tbsp light soy sauce • 1 tsp fresh ginger, grated •
green of 1 spring onion, finely chopped

SPRING ONION OIL
(MO HANH)
200 ml vegetable oil
• 1 bunch of spring onions, finely chopped

Heat the oil in the pan along with the spring
onion. Stir and remove immediately from the
heat so that the spring onion does not stick.

HERB SALAD
(RAU SONG)
Salad (lettuce, Iceberg lettuce, finely sliced cabbage) •
Coriander • Mint • Asian basil • Shiso • Spring onion

SWEET AND SOUR SAUCE
(SOT CHUA NGOT)

1 ripe tomato, finely chopped • 1 tbsp concentrated tomato paste • 1 lime
• 100 g brown sugar • 1 pinch of sea salt

Let the sugar cook in 200 ml of water until a syrup forms. Add the tomato and season
with a pinch of salt. Leave to simmer gently, covered. Finally, add the tomato paste and lime
juice for more flavour.

FRIED SHALLOTS
(HANH PHI)

200 ml vegetable oil • 5 shallots, in rings

Heat the oil and sauté the shallots until golden brown. Remove
the shallots with a slotted spoon and drain on kitchen paper.

PEANUT SAUCE
(SOT DAU PHONG)

1 tbsp unsalted, roasted peanuts, finely chopped • 2 stalks of lemongrass, finely chopped • 1 tsp red
curry paste • 100 ml coconut milk • 1 tbsp vegetable oil • pinch of brown sugar • pinch of sea salt

Sauté the lemongrass along with the curry paste in the oil. Add the coconut milk
and season with a pinch of sea salt and brown sugar. Add the peanuts.

179

THE FLAVOURS OF
VIETNAM

The choice of ingredients is absolutely crucial in Vietnamese cooking.

Freshness and quality are paramount, whether for the herbs

and spices, vegetables or fruit, or rice and noodles.

You'll find everything you need in an Asian supermarket and sometimes

even in your local supermarket. Because some ingredients may be less well

known we've made a list of the most important ones.

FRESH HERBS

Peppermint - Rau hung
Is known to us as regular mint. It can give a
fresh flavour to salads, for example.

Vietnamese mint - Rau ram
Mainly used in salads.
Stronger flavour than peppermint.

Lime leaf - La chanh
Lime leaf is used in chicken dishes,
such as chicken curry.

Coriander - Ngo / Rau mui
Coriander is usually eaten raw. It is
packed with vitamins A, B and C.
Finely chop and sprinkle it over soups
or stews just before serving.

Red shiso - Tia to
Has a strong aroma with hints of mint and
lemon.
Often used in rice soup and herb salads.

Asian basil - Rau que
This plant has a purple stem and
tastes strongly of anise.
Used in mixed salads and curries.

Wild betel leaf - La lot
Used to roll beef in before frying
or grilling. The leaf is never eaten raw.

Rice paddy herb - Ngo om
This herb is often used in stews,
curries, soups and fish broth.
Gives an edge to flavour.

FRESH HERBS

Spring onion - Hanh la
The white part is used for sautéing,
the green part as garnish.
Often used as garnish in soups.

Lemongrass - Sa
A common ingredient in Vietnamese cuisine.
Smells and tastes a lot like lemon.
Often used crushed or added whole to
flavour broths and marinades.

SPICES

Ginger - Gung
Ginger (yang) goes perfectly with fish and
seafood (yin). It brings balance to a dish.
Ginger is good for the blood circulation.

Turmeric - Nghe
Turmeric has a mildly bitter taste and a
strong aroma. It provides the yellow colour in
dishes, such as curries. Prevents infections.

Five-spice powder - Ngu vi huong
This powder is a blend of cinnamon,
star anise, cloves, black cardamom
and fennel seed.

Turmeric powder - Bone nghe
If you cannot find fresh turmeric,
you can use turmeric powder instead.

Annatto seeds - Hat dieu mau

Often used in curries and gives an
orange/red colour to a dish.
Slightly peppery flavour. Can be replaced
with paprika or cayenne powder.

Star anise - Hoi

Has a strong aniseed flavour and is
mainly used in meat dishes and soups.

Black peppercorns - Hat tieu den

An essential ingredient in many
Vietnamese dishes. The best pepper
in Vietnam can be found in Phu Quoc
and the Central Highlands.

Black cardamom - Thao qua

Is used in soups, such as pho.
Can be replaced with cloves.

Cinnamon - Que

Cinnamon is available in both
powder and stick form.

Clove - Dinh huong

Clove has a very dominant flavour.
The spice is often used in stews or soups.

Chilli pepper - Ot hiem
Very spicy pepper that is often
used in dipping sauces.
Only use in moderation.

Red chilli pepper - Ot sung
This pepper is moderately spicy and
is used in fish sauce vinaigrette.

Garlic - Toi
Is used in marinades, for frying or
in dipping sauces. Garlic is an antioxidant
and helps lower cholesterol.

Galangal root - Cu rieng
Is related to ginger. Tastes like ginger
and lemongrass. Delicious in salads and
barbecue marinade sauce.

FRUIT & VEGETABLES

Sweet potato - Khoai lang
The sweet potato is a starchy tuber.
Often used in curries and soups.

Morning glory - Rau muong
A daily vegetable in all of Vietnam.
Used in stir-fries, soups and salads.

Green papaya - Du du xanh

An essential ingredient in many
Vietnamese salads. A ripe papaya is dark
orange on the inside and is eaten as a fruit.

Green mustard leaf - Choisam / Cai ngot

Usually used in soups, but also in stir-fry dishes.
This leaf is seen as the yin in a dish and
is good for digestion. It is often balanced
with ginger, which is the yang.

Lime - Chanh

An essential ingredient in Vietnamese cuisine.
The leaves, zest and juice are used to give a
fresh flavour to dishes. Often used in curries,
soups, dips and salad dressings.

Shallot - Hanh tim

Often finely crushed and used in marinades
and sauces or deep-fried to garnish certain
dishes. Gives a nice flavour, especially
in caramelized dishes.

Watercress - Xa lach xoong

Often used in soups and salads.

Bean sprouts - Gia

Bean sprouts give a tasty and
crispy flavour to noodle dishes.
Often served as a side dish.

Rice flour - Bot gao
A flour made from rice.
Rice flour is used to make noodles,
rice sheets, crepes...

Rice sheets - Banh trang
There are various types of rice sheets.
Use them to make nem,
fresh spring rolls...

Rice vermicelli - Bun

Very fine rice vermicelli - Banh hoi

Flat rice vermicelli - Banh pho / Hu tieu
Available fresh or dried.

Rice flakes - Com Dep
Young sticky rice.

OTHER

Tofu - Dau hu
Is a popular substitute for meat and is often
used in Vietnam. It is made from soybeans
and has a white colour.

Banana leaf - La chuoi
Banana leaves are used to wrap fish
and meat before being steamed or grilled.
Or as a base in a steamer basket to
prevent food from sticking to the basket.

Soybean vermicelli - Mien / Bun tau
Used in nem, soups and stir-fries.

Black sesame seeds - Me den
Has a slightly nutty flavour and gives
a dish a crunchy texture.

Sesame seeds - Me trang
Light variation of black sesame seeds.

Coconut milk - Nuoc cot dua
Often used in curries and desserts.

Fish sauce - Nuoc mam
The most important sauce in Vietnam.
Is used in almost all dishes and dips.
It is rich in proteins and boosts immunity.

Soy sauce - Tuong
Light, salty soy sauce is used in salad
dressings. The darker, sweeter and thicker
soy sauce is used in more caramelly dishes.

INDEX

B

Baked sea bream fillet and dill *52*

Barbecue meat *34*

Beef and watercress salad *142*

Beef rolled in la lot leaves *140*

Brill fillet in banana leaf *160*

Broth of beef shank and lemongrass *84*

C

Chayote with eggs *130*

Clams with red curry *176*

Cooked snails *76*

Crispy scampi *56*

D

Deep-fried tofu with soy-lemon dressing *94*

Duck breast with five-spice powder *74*

Duck with yellow curry *158*

F

Fried rice noodles with vegetables *88*

Fried squid *64*

G

Green beans with beef and tomato *122*

Grilled cockles *120*

Grilled chicken with lime leaves *78*

Grilled pork belly with rice vermicelli *54*

Grilled quail *32*

L

Langoustines grilled on charcoal *62*

Lobster with yellow curry *168*

M

Mechelen Coucou with ginger *110*

Minced shrimp and squid on lemongrass stick *162*

Mixed vegetables in curry sauce *98*

Mussels with lemongrass *174*

N

Noodle soup with beef *44*

O

Omelette with scampi *112*

P

Pancake with scampi and pork belly *106*

Pink grapefruit salad with scampi *90*

Pumpkin with scampi *126*

Q

Quy Nhon fishcakes *128*

R

Red mullet with chicory *156*

Rice pancake filled with meat and mushrooms *46*

Rice soup with pigeon and mung beans *118*

S

Scallops *66*

Scampi with pepper and fish sauce *172*

Scampi wonton with soy dipping sauce *108*

Soup of ground scampi and mustard leaves *72*

Soup with tofu and tomato *92*

Spring rolls with tofu and vegetables *96*

Steamed sea bass *124*

Stewed aubergines *36*

Stew of tofu with red rice and vegetables *86*

Stuffed courgette with chicken and vegetables *104*

Sweet banana nem *146*

T

Tofu with lemongrass *132*

Tuna carpaccio *170*

V

Vietnamese sandwich *144*

Vietnamese spring rolls with meat and vegetables *50*

ACKNOWLEDGEMENTS

In writing this book, I embarked upon a wonderful journey with a number of people. It was an intense process, one from which I learned a lot and for which I am very grateful. In particular, I thank my publisher, Willy Faes, for believing in me; Sylvie D'Hoore for committing my words to paper so beautifully; Anh Du Thanh Khiem who helped me to articulate the Vietnamese culture and traditions; the people of Njam TV who give me the chance to showcase my country on television; my family and my Little Asia team who always support me in all situations; all guests of Little Asia, all of whom I love; Vietnam travel expert Chi Tran Thu Lan who always helps me to discover new sides to my country; the Vietnamese Buddhist Zen master Thay Thich Nhat Hanh who has inspired me greatly in recent years; and all the people I might have forgotten to mention but who are equally important.

While this cookbook is inspired entirely by Vietnam, I also want to express my gratitude for all the chances I've been given in the last 29 years in Belgium. To all the residents of Wichelen who gave us an unforgettable welcome when we arrived in Belgium in 1986 and all the people who believed in me and who helped me to build my life here: thank you.

Quyên

Restaurant Little Asia, rue Sainte-Catherine 8, 1000 Brussels, www.littleasia.be

© 2016 Publisher Purple Pumpkin, Kontich, Belgium /
Aerial Media Company, Tiel, The Netherlands

ISBN 9789402601244

TEXT
Sylvie D'Hoore

TRANSLATION
Tradas
Editor English text: Danny Guinan, Wordforword

EDITORIAL TEAM
Purple Pumpkin

PHOTOGRAPHY
Lucas van Lieshout, Steven Cuypers, Tran Van Thinh, Koen De Leeuw,
Jef De Schutter, Eric Boon, Sylvie D'Hoore, Dublju, Shutterstock, 123rf

GRAPHIC DESIGN & STYLING
Violeta Kazakova

RECIPES
Truong Thi Quyên

EDITOR-IN-CHIEF
Charlotte Van den Langenbergh

PRINTING
Albe De Coker, Antwerp

Thanks to Van Uytsel, Pomax, Serax, Point-Virgule.

The moral rights of Truong Thi Quyên to be identified as the author of this work has been
asserted in accordance with the Copyright, Designs and Patents Act of 1988.

Conversion Charts

Here are rounded-off equivalents between the metric system and the traditional systems used in the UK and United States to measure weight and volume.

Farenheit	Celsius	Gas Mark
275º F	140º C	gas mark 1-cool
300º F	150º C	gas mark 2
325º F	165º C	gas mark 3-very moderate
350º F	180º C	gas mark 4-moderate
375º F	190º C	gas mark 5
400º F	200º C	gas mark 6-moderately hot
425º F	220º C	gas mark 7- hot
450º F	230º C	gas mark 9
475º F	240º C	gas mark 10- very hot

Metric to US Conversions

1 milliliter	1/5 teaspoon
5 ml	1 teaspoon
15 ml	1 tablespoon
30 ml	1 fluid oz.
100 ml	3.4 fluid oz.
240 ml	1 cup
1 liter	34 fluid oz
1 liter	4.2 cups
1 liter	2.1 pints
1 liter	1.06 quarts
1 liter	0.26 gallon
1 gram	0.035 ounce
100 grams	3.5 ounces
500 grams	1.10 pounds
1 kilogram	2.205 pounds
1 kilogram	35 oz.